For my father, who shared with me
on those early mornings many years ago
the thrill of watching NASA launch its first men
into space, and for encouraging in me
an interest in all things science.

And for Paul—thank you for being in my life.

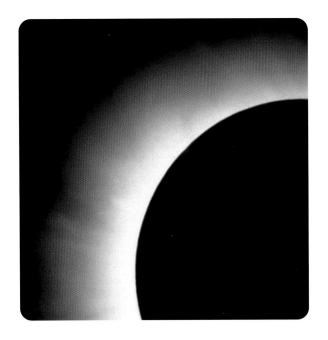

CONTENTS

INTRODUCTION

Have you ever been on vacation, at the seashore, perhaps, or a desert resort in New Mexico—somewhere away from city lights—and looked up, seemingly for the first time, at a sky full of stars?

"Whoa!" you say to your spouse or buddy or family member. "Look at all the stars!"

"Yeah," he or she answers. "Hey, I can see the Big Dipper."

"Oh, yeah! So can I." And then there's silence for a while. Until . . .

"What's the really bright star over there?" your spouse asks.

You shake your head. "I don't know."

"Maybe it's the North Star," your spouse suggests, trying to be helpful.

"What's the North Star?"

"Well, it's a bright star . . . in the north . . . isn't it?"

And there's more silence, while you both gaze upward, admiring the view but wishing you knew more about what you were looking at.

Sound familiar? You're not alone. People have been fascinated by the stars for thousands of years. And, while our methods of observing have changed (no telescopes or orbiting spacecraft in the old days), our reasons for wanting to know more about the celestial vault above us haven't. Our strong sense of curiosity, our need to know where we came from, how we got here, and what the future holds—and whether there's anyone else out there like us: these are what drive us to explore the mysteries of the universe.

Until fairly recently, astronomy was the province of serious scientists—Einstein, for instance, and Newton, who spent their lives cooking up concepts like the theory of relativity and why things fall down instead of up. Amateur astronomy was introduced in the twentieth century, but it was largely practiced by pale, sleep-deprived guys who spent their nights studying planets (when they weren't studying math) and hunting for comets. Even if you were interested in stargazing, you needed a telescope, didn't you? And they were expensive and much too complicated for those of us without genius-level IQs.

Things have changed. Oh, serious scientists still spend their lives arguing over the complexities of black holes and whether Pluto is really a planet, but, today, anyone with an interest in it can indulge in stargazing. Telescopes have become better, cheaper, and easier to use (although you can stargaze perfectly well without one); astronomy clubs and websites abound; and a wealth of information, in the form of magazines and books like this one, can be found in bookstores. No longer just for scientists, astronomy has become a mainstream hobby.

This book won't tell you everything you've always wanted to know about astronomy, but it will explain how to tell a star from a planet, what those dark blotches on the Moon are, what causes the aurora, and how to safely observe the Sun. It will tell you how to read a star map and navigate your way around the sky, where and when the next total eclipse will occur, and how to photograph the constellations. You'll find out what you'll need to get started on your way to becoming a backyard astronomer, so you can begin observing tonight. And you'll find forty-six observing projects to help you turn "What's that up there?" into "Hey, there's that double cluster in Perseus." Plus a whole lot more.

So, the next time your spouse or buddy or family member asks, "What's that really bright star over there?" you can answer, "Oh, that's not a star, that's Venus. And see that fuzzy patch below those three bright stars? That's the Orion Nebula. And over there . . . ."

First, a Little Background

You're forgiven if you thought astronomy was a fairly recent science. Most of us weren't even aware of the subject until the Sixties, when America and the U.S.S.R. started hurling rockets into space as fast as they could, to be the first to place a man on the Moon. There's an assumption that astronomy is high-tech, what with the International Space Station orbiting the Earth, rovers rambling about on Mars, and space-based telescopes taking pictures of galaxies far, far, away. It's science fiction become science reality (although we have a long, *long* way to go before we'll be "going where no one has gone before").

And yet, the truth is that astronomy is the oldest of sciences. People have been looking up at the sky for thousands of years. The very earliest stargazers saw pictures in the stars: warriors and dragons and bears. They made up stories to explain the rising and setting of the Sun and the Moon and how the Earth and sky came to be. The movements of the Sun and the stars told farmers when to plant and harvest their crops, and nomadic tribes when to expect warmer weather and the return of herds to their summer feeding grounds. Mariners navigated by the stars, using the constellations as stellar road maps.

Four thousand years ago, stargazers in Mesopotamia were studying the skies and writing down their observations on cuneiform tablets. They were the first to divide the sky into constellations and identify the zodiac. About the same time, Chinese astronomers recorded solar eclipses, invented their own constellations, and designed a calendar based on the yearly cycle of the shadows cast by the Sun. The Egyptians were busy, too, devising lunar calendars and building their amazing pyramids.

It was the Greeks who began to turn astronomy into the science we recognize today. They had already developed the idea that the stars were fixed in a celestial sphere that turned around the Earth, Sun, and planets, but it was Ptolemy, in the second century AD, who envisioned a model of the solar system with the Earth at the center. (Although Aristotle was actually the first to propose the geocentric system, in about 350 BC, it was Ptolemy who got the credit for it, because his theory could be used to predict the motions

The Chinese Celestial Sphere

The Chinese have a long history of studying the stars and keeping records of their observations. They are believed to have been the first to devise an astronomical instrument—a bamboo pole stuck into the ground to measure time and the seasons by the position of the Sun's shadow. More sophisticated devices came along later. This celestial globe, for instance, built in 1673, was used to determine the positions of the stars, regardless of the weather or time of day. The globe is part of an impressive collection of ancient Chinese instruments at the Ancient Observatory (Guanxiangtai) in Beijing.

of the planets against the starry background.) Ptolemy's model persisted for almost 1,500 years, until 1543, when a Polish scholar, Nicholas Copernicus, started to unravel this concept with his suggestion that the Earth actually orbited the Sun.

By this time, European astronomers had long since taken over all things astronomical. Galileo, an Italian, turned the science on its head when he became the first to aim the newly invented telescope at the sky. Suddenly, he was seeing things no one had seen before: mountains on the Moon, moons circling Jupiter, millions of stars in the Milky Way. His observations also led him to agree with Copernicus and into trouble with the Church, which was not amused by his heretical theories (according to the Church, Earth was at the center of the universe). Although later scientists, such as German mathematician Johannes Kepler and French philosopher Pierre Gassendi shared Galileo's belief in a Copernican system, it was a long time before it became the widely held and publicly accepted model we know today.

With the introduction of new theories and observations in the seventeenth to twentieth centuries from scientists like Kepler (planet orbits are elliptical), William Herschel (the Sun moves in space, first to map the Milky Way system), Friedrich Bessel (first to estimate the distance to a nearby star) and Edwin Hubble (identified stars in what we now call the Andromeda Galaxy, which he showed was very, very far away), Earth began to assume its place in the cosmos, as a planet circling a middling Sun in a vast, vast universe.

OMENS AND SUPERSTITION

Early astronomy was more about superstition and mythology than what we today would call science. Astronomy and astrology were closely tied (although they aren't anymore; never confuse the two if you don't want to receive a tongue-lashing from a dedicated astronomer), and kings and emperors relied on their royal astronomer/astrologers to inform them when the stars were favorable for going to war or getting married. Comets and eclipses were dire omens. The sight of a "broom star" (a Chinese term for a comet) drifting across the heavens could presage the downfall of a monarchy, and the failure to predict a solar eclipse could mean the downfall of an astronomer.

One of those unfortunate monarchs was King Harold of England. In 1066, soon after his coronation, a comet appeared in the sky. It was Halley's Comet, making one of its cyclic seventy-six-year appearances. Roughly five months later, William of Normandy's longboats made landfall on England's southern coast, and Harold was killed in the Battle of Hastings. The story of the Norman invasion is told in the Bayeux Tapestry (a panel is shown above), a 230-foot (70-m) long embroidered "document" commissioned by William's half-brother, Bishop Odo of Bayeux, shortly after the battle.

Our Place in Space

If you could climb aboard a spaceship and fly to a viewpoint outside the Milky Way galaxy, you would have a difficult time picking out our solar system. First of all, our Sun is only one of roughly 100 *billion* stars in this galactic city we call home, and it's located in the suburbs, an outer spiral arm about two-thirds of the way from Milky Way Central, the big, bright bulge in the center. There, at the hub, stars are packed tightly together (less than half a light-year apart), whereas the nearest star in our neighborhood, Proxima Centauri, is 4.2 light-years away.

What's a light-year? It's the distance light travels in a year: 5.9 trillion miles (9.5 trillion km), at 186,000 miles (299,000 km) per *second*. We use light-years to describe distances in space because they're so vast that describing them in miles or kilometers is impractical; we would have to add too many zeroes to every number. Although we speak of it in terms of time, a light-year actually refers to distance. When we say that Proxima Centauri is 4.2. light-years away, it means that it takes 4.2 years for the light from that star to travel to us here on Earth. How far is that in miles? Well, multiply 4.2 by 5.9 trillion (9.5 trillion km), and that's how far away the nearest star is—roughly 24.8 trillion miles (39.9 trillion km).

The Milky Way from Earth

Yes, you can see our home galaxy from Earth (or part of it, anyway), but you need a dark location away from city lights to see the spill of stars across the night sky. Observe the Milky Way in both summer and winter. Notice that it seems brighter in the summer? That's because the Earth is turned toward the center of the galaxy, and we're seeing the light from the bright central bulge. In the winter, Earth is turned away from the center, and we're looking outward, across the Perseus Arm, into an area of fewer stars.

Some stars and deep-sky objects (you'll learn more about these in Chapter Five), such as those photographed by the Hubble Space Telescope, are so distant, that it takes millions—even billions—of years for their light to reach us. Take the star Deneb, for instance, in the constellation Cygnus, 1,600 light-years away. You can see Deneb from your backyard. But you're seeing it as it was 1,600 years ago, because it takes that long for its light to reach Earth. In fact, if Deneb suddenly died out today, you wouldn't know about it for another 1,600 years. In a sense, when you look at the sky, you're looking back in time.

The Milky Way isn't the only galaxy whirling about in space, of course. It's part of a group of galaxies, which is part of a bigger group of galaxies, which is part of a still larger group . . . well, you get the idea. It's an inconceivably immense Universe, and trying to comprehend it can seriously hurt the brain.

Sun

You Are Here

If we could look down on our galaxy from a point in space, this is what we'd see: a bright, central bulge, glowing with tightly packed stars, surrounded by glittering spiral arms. Where are we? Our solar system is about two-thirds of the way out from the center, on the inside edge of what is called the Orion Arm.

THE SOLAR SYSTEM BY NUMBERS

4.6	Age of the solar system, in billions of years
9	Number of planets
1,429	Diameter of Pluto, smallest planet, in miles (2,390 km)
88,793	Diameter of Jupiter, largest planet, in miles (142,980 km)
7,909	Diameter of Earth, in miles (12,756 km)
3.6	Average distance of Pluto from the Sun, in *billions* of miles (5.9 billion km)
36	Average distance of Mercury from the Sun, in *millions* of miles (57 million km)
365.25	Time, in days, for Earth to orbit the Sun
248.5	Time, in years, for Pluto to orbit the Sun

Solar Satellites

Nine planets circle the Sun, along with an assortment of moons and asteroids, in a disk-like plane. Speeding around the inside tracks, closest to the Sun, are the four *terrestrial* planets: Mercury, Venus, Earth, and Mars, small, rocky worlds similar in size and composition to the Earth. Plodding about the Sun in the outside lanes are the giant planets: Jupiter, Saturn, Uranus, and Neptune—huge, gaseous planets that resemble Jupiter. And then there's Pluto, a small, icy planet with a titled orbit, whose status as a planet has been debated. On the fringes of the solar system are a ring of icy objects called the Kuiper Belt and a vast sphere of comets called the Oort Cloud. *Planets and orbits not drawn to scale.*

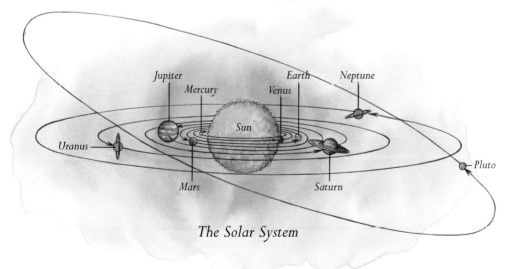

The Solar System

CHAPTER ONE
GETTING STARTED

In the upcoming chapters, you'll be reading about all the wonderful sights to see up there in the night sky: the Moon, the
planets, the constellations, galaxies, and nebulas. You'll want to
get out there and start looking for them. But how do you begin?

That's what this chapter is for. Here's where you'll find out
how to observe before you read about what to observe.

The Big Dipper is probably the most easily recognized star pattern in the night sky, although it's not a constellation. It's an asterism, a pattern of stars, part of the constellation of Ursa Major. Follow the curve of the Dipper's "handle," from the "bowl" to its last star—the next bright star you come to is Arcturus.

Getting to Know the Sky

As a newcomer to stargazing, you may be thinking that the first thing you need to do is buy a telescope. Your enthusiasm is understandable. After all, you've seen the glossy calendars and coffee-table books with their photos of multicolored nebulas, spiraling galaxies, and finely spun Saturnian rings. You want to see them for real. Now.

But where would you look for these galaxies, these nebulas? And which one of those bright specks up there is Saturn, anyway? You see the problem?

Rushing out to buy a telescope at this point is a little like buying a bicycle before you even know how to crawl. It will sit gathering dust until you learn, and you may find, when you do begin to ride, that the bike you bought is not the bike you want or need. Worse, you may discover that you don't even like bike-riding. And so the bicycle goes back into the attic or outside at your next garage sale.

So, what *is* the first step?

Getting to know the sky. You can spend a considerable amount of time identifying constellations, observing the motions of the planets, studying the phases of the Moon, and much, much more—with the naked eye. There's plenty to see if you know where to look and what to look for. Remember those early Mesopotamians? They spent thousands of years studying the skies—and not one of them had a telescope.

Start by learning the constellations. Look ahead to the sky maps in Chapter Six, pick a star pattern from the map for the current month (choose one with a few bright stars, rather than a lot of faint stars), then go outside and see whether you can find it. Keep doing this for a while; in time, you'll find that you won't need the maps to find Andromeda or Hercules. You'll know that Cygnus won't be visible in February and that the Big

Dipper never dips below the horizon at mid-northern latitudes. Then move on to Chapter Three and learn about the planets. Over time, the sky and its movements will become very familiar.

Getting to know the sky with the unaided eye can help you appreciate the beauty and mystery of the cosmos. It will also help immeasurably when it comes time to add optics, because you'll know where to point that telescope or pair of binoculars.

Observing Tips

Ready to start stargazing? Here are a few tips to help make your session more comfortable and enjoyable.

Check the conditions. Is it hazy or cloudy? Try another night. Is the sky lit by a bright full Moon? Depending on what you're observing, this may not be a problem. But a full Moon washes out the sky, and you may not be able to see much. Wait for another night, or observe before the Moon rises or after it sets. Check out an astronomy website, such as *www.skyandtele scope.com* for that night's viewing highlights.

Get dark adapted. It takes the eyes about thirty minutes to become fully dark adapted; that is, to adjust to the darkness. The longer you stay in the dark, without looking at bright light, the more you will be able to see. Spend about fifteen minutes getting used to the darkness before you start your observing session. Turn off the lights in the house, too, in case you have to come inside for any reason.

WHAT CAN YOU SEE?

The naked eye can see about 3,000 stars, and most of the eighty-eight constellations, depending on the darkness of the sky. Here, Orion rises above the trees on a wintry night.

Three bright stars form the handle of the Big Dipper. Binoculars reveal the bright star in the middle to be two stars: Mizar (bottom) and fainter Alcor (top).

Although the double cluster in Perseus is visible through binoculars, a 4-inch (100-mm) telescope brings out the true beauty—and colors—of the stars.

With the Naked Eye

- Constellations and asterisms (how many is determined by your latitude; people in the Southern Hemisphere never see the far northern constellations and vice versa)
- The Milky Way (in a dark sky, away from city lights)
- Mercury, Venus, Mars, Jupiter, and Saturn
- Major features on the Moon
- Satellites, meteors, and meteor showers
- Bright comets
- Lunar and solar eclipses (Be sure to use a proper viewing filter for solar eclipses!)
- Auroras
- A handful of bright star clusters
- The Andromeda Galaxy
- The Large and Small Clouds of Magellan (Southern Hemisphere only)

With Binoculars

All of the preceding (except meteors and auroras), in more detail, plus

- Some double stars
- Close-up views of the Milky Way
- Up to four of Jupiter's moons
- Major craters and mountain ranges on the Moon
- Transits of Mercury and Venus (with proper solar filters)
- Sunspots (with solar filters)
- Some nebulas
- Fainter star clusters

With a Small Telescope (4-inch/100-mm)

All of the preceding, plus

- Rings of Saturn
- Moons of Saturn
- Features on Mars (sometimes)
- Phases of Venus and Mercury
- Belts of Jupiter
- Hundreds more craters on the Moon, plus other harder-to-see details
- Colors in stars
- Many more nebulas and star clusters
- Galaxies

Use a red light. Once you've been outside in the dark for a while, the last thing you want to do is turn on a white-light flashlight to read your star map. You'll destroy your dark adaptation and will have to start all over again. A red-light flashlight will allow you to see what you're doing without losing your night vision. You can buy a red LED flashlight (see Resources on page 150), or you can easily make one of your own by covering a regular flashlight with red cellophane, gel, or paper or by painting the bulb with red nail polish.

Always use a red-light flashlight when observing—it will ensure you stay dark adapted.

Dress warmly. Nights can be cool, even in the summer. And you won't be moving around much. Have a thermos of hot coffee or hot chocolate handy, and, if you find your fingers and toes going numb, do some running on the spot once in a while to get your circulation going (be sure to move away from any equipment; you don't want to incur the wrath of an astronomer whose telescope is bumped after she's carefully aligned it). If you're stargazing in winter, go inside every half hour or so to warm up. In the summer, have insect repellant on hand.

Find a dark location. This can be tricky, especially in the city, where bright lights are ubiquitous. Find the darkest corner of your yard, away from streetlights or other neighboring light sources, with an unobstructed view of the sky. Alternatively, head for a neighborhood park (but only if this option is safe). You may never find an ideal place to stargaze, but that's okay. Make the best of the situation you have. You may be surprised, over time, at how much you can see. If the yard is out of the question (or you don't have one), join an observing club and stargaze with other members; they're certain to know where the good views are—and you'll have company, to boot.

Use a lounge chair. Standing around gazing up will cramp your neck before long. Reclining in a lounge chair will be much more comfortable.

Use averted vision. The edges of your eyes are more sensitive to dim light. Averting your vision slightly—looking at an object out of the corner of your eye—will help you see objects that are invisible to the eye when viewed straight on.

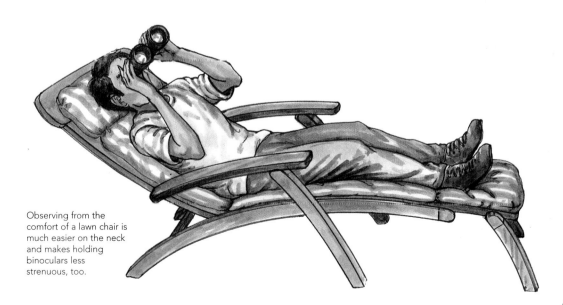

Observing from the comfort of a lawn chair is much easier on the neck and makes holding binoculars less strenuous, too.

Venus and a crescent Moon adorn the early morning sky. Venus is sometimes called the "Morning Star."

Use binoculars, if you have them. Any pair will improve the view. Aim them at the Moon or a planet (Jupiter, for instance). Or train them on an object you can barely see with the naked eye. You'll be surprised at the difference in what you can see.

Keep an observing log. It doesn't have to be elaborate, just a quick jotting down of the evening's sights. Think of it as a kind of celestial diary. You may find, in time, that your notes become more detailed, describing weather conditions and how much more vivid, say, the bands of color on Jupiter looked tonight compared to the last time you viewed the planet. And, if you get into astrophotography, your log will become a convenient place to record your efforts—what worked, and what didn't. Looking back on it months or years later will remind you of how much your observing skills have improved.

When the Atmosphere is Not Your Friend

Have you ever wondered why the Hubble Space Telescope is, well . . . out in space? After all, we have plenty of observatories with telescopes down here on Earth. Some of them, like the Canada-France-Hawaii Telescope, are perched on mountaintops (Hawaii's Mauna Kea, in this case), high above the smog and clouds that obscure the view of observers at lower elevations. The view ought to be pretty good from up there, right?

Not all the time. And it's because of something called *atmospheric turbulence*—that is, turbulence caused by, yes, Earth's atmosphere.

Got a pair of binoculars kicking around? By all means, employ them. Even a small pair used for birdwatching will bring the stars in closer. When you're ready to find out more, check out Chapter Ten for advice on using and buying binoculars for astronomy.

Generally speaking, our atmosphere is a good thing. It's what makes the sky blue and green things grow. It's what gives us spectacular sunsets, rainbows, and cool breezes on hot summer days. It's what allows us to breathe.

The bad news is that the atmosphere can get in the way when you're observing, turning what seems like a clear, calm night into a boiling, seething cauldron of air that distorts whatever you're looking at through the telescope. Have you ever been in the desert and seen those waves of heat rising from the ground on a blistering summer day? Did you notice that objects in the distance seemed to wobble and shimmer and never quite come into focus? Atmospheric turbulence does that to objects seen through the telescope; they blur together and dance about, making it impossible to see details.

Astronomers use the word "seeing" to describe viewing conditions through a telescope. On a night when stars and other objects shimmer and bounce around a lot, you'll hear them say "the seeing was bad." A good night for seeing is when the atmosphere is calm and objects look clear and steady through the scope. Rare is the night when some turbulence doesn't mar the view, but you can take some steps to alleviate it.

- At least an hour before your observing session, bring your telescope outside and let it "cool down." A scope that's warmer than the air around it sheds heat, generating turbulence of its own.
- Observe later at night, when the heat of the day has had a chance to dissipate. (Although some observers suggest going out immediately after sunset, do both and see what happens.)
- Avoid observing objects when they are close to the horizon. You're looking through more air at an object near the horizon than when it's straight overhead.
- Take note of the weather. Changing patterns of high and low pressure tend to swirl the air around; seeing may be better when the weather has remained unchanged for a while.
- If you can get to higher ground, this also helps.

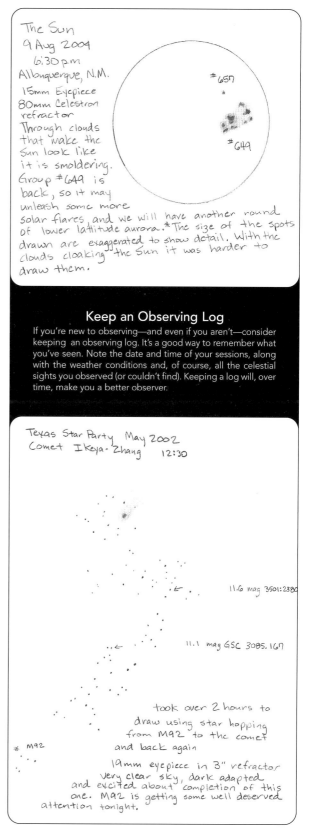

The Sun
9 Aug 2004
6:30 p.m
Albuquerque, N.M.
15mm Eyepiece
80mm Celestron refractor
Through clouds that make the Sun look like it is smoldering. Group #649 is back, so it may unleash some more solar flares, and we will have another round of lower latitude aurora. *The size of the spots drawn are exaggerated to show detail. With the clouds cloaking the Sun it was harder to draw them.

#657
#649

Keep an Observing Log

If you're new to observing—and even if you aren't—consider keeping an observing log. It's a good way to remember what you've seen. Note the date and time of your sessions, along with the weather conditions and, of course, all the celestial sights you observed (or couldn't find). Keeping a log will, over time, make you a better observer.

Texas Star Party   May 2002
Comet Ikeya-Zhang   12:30

11.6 mag 3501:2380
11.1 mag GSC 3085.167

took over 2 hours to draw using star hopping from M92 to the comet and back again

19mm eyepiece in 3" refractor Very clear sky, dark adapted and excited about completion of this one. M92 is getting some well deserved attention tonight.

M92

BLINDED BY THE LIGHT

Many of us never truly see a proper night sky. From within the city (where most of us live), we can see the brighter stars, but there are thousands more twinkling beyond the glowing yellow aura cast by city lights.

That glow is called light pollution. You may have seen pictures of North America taken from space—pictures showing a grid of glittering lights stretching coast to coast from southern Canada to Mexico (see right). In some areas, the patches of light are so thickly packed, you'd be hard pressed to find a glimpse of darkness.

You'll hear astronomers grumble about light pollution, and if you stick with stargazing, before long, you'll be grumbling, too. There's nothing quite as breathtaking as a really dark sky, not dotted but dusted with stars. Once you've seen a sky full of stars, a city sky pales in comparison—literally.

Now You See Them, Now You Don't

If you live in the city, you're probably acquainted with the pale, light-polluted sort of sky seen in the photo on the right. Only away from city lights can you truly appreciate the stellar beauty of a dark, star-filled sky. These two images show the same section of sky. The photo on the left was taken from a rural site in central Vermont, the one on the right from the photographer's backyard in suburban Boston.

Even more frustrating is knowing that much of the light shining throughout the city is wasted and unnecessary. Street lamps waste light by casting it sideways and up, instead of just down; businesses illuminate empty parking lots; porch lights stay on all night. All this burning light wastes energy, too. (Didn't your mother always tell you to turn off the light when you leave a room?)

If you're interested in finding out how to mitigate light pollution or in helping to advance awareness of the problem, you can check out the website of the International Dark Sky Association at *www.darksky.org*. The site, which includes information on outdoor lighting regulations and where to find a dark sky in your area, links to affiliate sites in several countries in North America, Europe, the Mediterranean, and Asia.

Night Lights

Assembled from hundreds of satellite images, this mosaic of the Earth at night shows with shimmering clarity where the world's population resides. Bright patches of light are spread like lichen over the United States and southern Canada, Europe, and Asia, with only Africa, Australia, and South America offering areas of still-dark skies.

CHAPTER TWO
THE MOON

All right, so you've pulled out the lawn chair, armed yourself with a good pair of binoculars and a thermos of coffee, and found a corner in the yard with an unobstructed view of the sky. What should you observe first?

How about the Moon? An ideal subject for beginner stargazers, the Moon is bright and conspicuous (unless it's a new Moon), and details on its surface are easy to see, even with the naked eye. Who hasn't scrutinized the dark blotches, for instance, and wondered what they were? Or puzzled over those bright lines radiating from a point resembling the stem end of a cantaloupe? Lift a pair of binoculars to your eyes, and the view gets even better, as more detail pops into focus.

Another reason the Moon is a good place to start? It's immensely rewarding. Unlike stars, which look like pinpoints to the naked eye and slightly brighter pinpoints through a telescope, the Moon can keep you busy for years. For very little effort, you receive a lot of gratification.

First, a Little Background

As moons go, Earth's is not the largest (it's the fifth largest; Ganymede, one of Jupiter's numerous moons, has the honor of being in the top spot), but, at one-quarter the diameter of Earth, it beats every other moon except Charon, Pluto's moon, for being the largest in relation to its mother planet. Although Ganymede and Titan, which places second on the size scale, may be bigger, they're tiny in relation to their mother planets, Jupiter and Saturn, respectively. This size relationship makes our Moon pretty unusual. In fact, some astronomers consider the Earth and Moon a double planet system.

Where did the Moon come from? After much debate, the currently accepted theory is that it was formed about 4.5 billion years ago, when a rampant space object the size of Mars smashed into the young Earth and knocked a chunk of it into space. The debris, caught in Earth's gravity, eventually coalesced into an orbiting moon.

The early solar system was a rough place, however, and for millions of years after its formation, the Moon suffered countless hits from comets, meteoroids, and other space debris. Some of these impacts were so forceful, they caused lava to well up from below the Moon's crust and flood the surface, forming the huge dark patches we see from Earth. Smaller hits, less powerful but more numerous, filled the remaining landscape with thousands upon thousands of craters.

Nothing major has collided with the Moon for roughly 100 million years, which means that what you see is pretty much what you'll ever get. Other than a few late-comer asteroid strikes, the Moon hasn't changed in about three billion years, unlike the Earth, whose geological activity redecorates its surface on a regular basis. There's no water on the Moon, and, without an atmosphere to provide some insulation, it suffers extreme temperature changes, rising to more than 250°F (123°C) in the day and plunging to at least −380°F (−233°C) at night. The Apollo astronauts, bounding around on the Moon's surface, found it an inhospitable, dead, gray world, a mausoleum of rock and stone.

And yet, as seen from Earth, the Moon is a subject for poets and lovers, who speak of its silver beams, white fire, and pearly light. It's true; a luminous full Moon on a warm summer night is a romantic sight. Lovely as it is, however, the full Moon is not an observer's friend—even if you're observing the Moon. Its brightness obliterates the view of the surrounding sky and makes its own features appear flat and washed out. A better time to observe the Moon is when only part of it is lit.

Glitter Path
The white light of a full Moon spills over the ocean, creating what is called a glitter path. Lovely as it is, a full Moon is not an observer's friend.

Phases of the Moon

If the Moon's face seems familiar and unchanging to you, that's because it is. We only ever see the same side of the Moon, the near side, which, as you might expect, is the side nearest the Earth. The far side of the Moon, the side consistently turned away from the Earth, can only be seen from space. Why do we only see the same side? Because the Moon takes the same amount of time to circle the Earth as it does to rotate once on its axis: that is, 27.3 days. As it revolves, half of the Moon is always lit by the Sun. The illuminated parts we see are called *phases*, and they change as the Moon orbits the Earth. One complete pass through the phases takes 29.5 days and is called a *lunar cycle*.

IT'S JUST A PHASE

As the Moon orbits the Earth, half of it is always lit by the Sun. The lit portion we see from Earth, however, changes according to the Moon's position. These are called phases. When the Moon is between the Sun and the Earth, and its near side faces away from the Sun, it's called a new Moon. When the Moon is on the opposite side of the Earth from the Sun, it's called a full Moon. When it's halfway between each of these two positions, the Moon is in its quarter phases.

Why isn't there a solar eclipse every month at new Moon or a lunar eclipse at full Moon? Because the Earth, Sun, and Moon are not usually lined up in space, and they have to be in exact alignment for an eclipse to occur, something that doesn't happen very often. (For more on eclipses and when to see them, see Chapter Eight and the Appendix.)

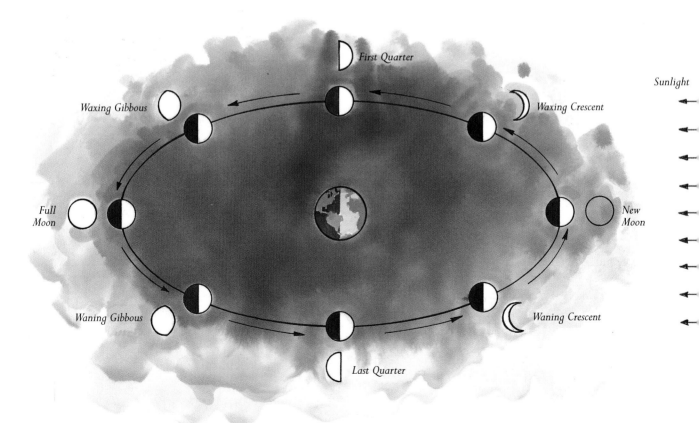

The lunar cycle begins with the *new Moon*, that is, when the Sun illuminates the far side of the Moon and the near side is in darkness. The new Moon traverses the sky during the day, rising and setting with the Sun. You can't see the new Moon.

As the days pass, the Moon begins to wax, meaning that the illuminated section of the Moon grows larger. It will also start to lag behind the Sun, rising later than the Sun each night and setting after the Sun each day. A few days after new Moon, early in the evening, a crescent will appear over the western horizon. Over the next seven days, it gradually increases in size (and sets a little later) until it reaches what is called *first quarter*—which actually looks like a half Moon. Confused? Remember, we only ever see half the Moon. And half of that (the illuminated part we see), therefore, is a quarter of the full globe. But astronomers call it first quarter because, at this point, the Moon is about one-quarter through its lunar cycle (which, if you remember, takes 29.5 days to complete). At this point, the Moon is rising at about noon and setting around midnight.

About a week after first quarter, the Moon reaches its *full* phase, rising as the Sun sets and setting as the Sun rises. Halfway through the lunar cycle, the Moon is positioned directly opposite the Sun and its near side is fully lit. Now it begins to wane—its lit portion growing smaller—as it starts to rise later. By *third quarter* (now the other "half of the half" is lit)—about twenty-two days after the new Moon— it rises at about midnight and sets near noon. (This is when you can see a daylight Moon early in the morning. It's also when you'll see bleary-eyed Moon-gazers stumbling into work; they've been up well before dawn, observing a phase of the Moon that most of us never see.) Seven days later, the cycle ends and a new Moon is born. Between the four major phases, the

When a Quarter is a Half

One quarter through its 29.5-day lunar cycle, the seven-day-old, first-quarter Moon appears as a half Moon. First quarter is a good time to observe features along the *terminator*, the line that divides the night side of the Moon from the day side. Here, shadows cast from the Sun clearly delineate the craters Ptolemaeus, Alphonsus, and Arzachel at the center of the terminator.

Moon passes through crescent and *gibbous* phases (when it's a little larger than half). The crescent Moons fall between new and first quarter (when the Moon is waxing) and last quarter and new (when it's waning). The gibbous Moons fall between first quarter and full and full and last quarter.

Earthshine

Odd though it seems, the Moon shines with no light of its own—its brightness is merely borrowed from the Sun. Occasionally, however, the Moon is ever-so-slightly illuminated by sunlight bouncing off the Earth, a phenomenon called *Earthshine*. Watch for it the next time the Moon is in a crescent phase. You'll see the bright rind of the sun-lit crescent cupping a faintly glowing, Earth-lit disk—the night side of the Moon.

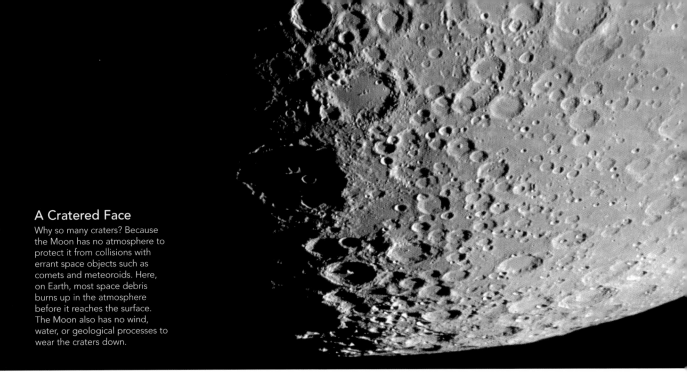

A Cratered Face

Why so many craters? Because the Moon has no atmosphere to protect it from collisions with errant space objects such as comets and meteoroids. Here, on Earth, most space debris burns up in the atmosphere before it reaches the surface. The Moon also has no wind, water, or geological processes to wear the craters down.

Features of the Moon

Even with the naked eye, it's easy to see that the Moon's surface is made up of two distinct landscapes: the dark lava plains and the brighter areas that cover the rest of the Moon. Still, until Galileo turned his telescope to the skies in 1609, no one knew exactly what those light and dark areas were. Astronomers in those days (including Galileo) assumed that the dark blotches were seas, so they named them *maria* (plural for *mare*, the Latin word for seas). The bright patches? Well, that was anyone's guess.

Imagine Galileo's surprise when his telescope showed him a close-up of the Moon's surface. Not only were there no seas, but the bright patches turned out to be craters, which quickly dispelled the firmly held notion that the Moon was a smooth, uniform celestial body.

A Tour of the Moon

You may find it helpful to follow our tour of the Moon by referring to A Map of the Moon on pages 28 and 29.

Maria

The maria are impact basins, huge roughly circular depressions that filled with lava erupting through the Moon's crust. Probably the best-known of the maria is Mare Tranquilitatis (Sea of Tranquility), where the Apollo 11 lunar lander touched down in 1969 and Neil Armstrong became the first person in history to walk on another world. Just above it is Mare Serenitatis (Sea of Serenity), and below and to the east is Mare Fecunditatis (Sea of Fertility). Rounding out the complement of maria in the Moon's eastern half are Mare Nectaris, a small mare to the southwest of Fecunditatis, and Mare Crisium (Sea of Crises), a distinctive circular mare off by itself in the east.

The maria in the Moon's western half are more difficult to distinguish from one another, as they all appear to be melded together into one large mass. The largest chunk of this mass is claimed by Oceanus Procellarum (Ocean of Storms). No mere mare, Procellarum sprawls over the western-most part of the Moon, as far as the limb (the limb is the edge of the Moon). Below Procellarum is a smaller circular patch; this is Mare Humorum (Sea of Moisture). East of it is Mare Nubium (Sea of Clouds) and straight up, to the north of Procellarum, is Mare Imbrium (Sea of Rains), at 700 miles (1,100 km) in diameter, one of the largest of the Moon's circular impact basins.

Craters

Not to be confused with volcanic craters, such as those found on Earth, lunar craters are *impact craters*, formed by hits from cosmic debris. (You can see an impact crater here on Earth by visiting Meteor Crater in Arizona.) Hundreds of thousands of them make up what are called the *lunar highlands*, the brighter areas on the Moon's surface that we can see from Earth.

While the maria are visible with the naked eye, you'll need some magnification to see the craters. Binoculars will show you the major craters; a small telescope will reveal many more. To get the best view of the craters, however, you'll need to observe when the Moon is not full—about three days after new Moon until three days before full, and three days after full Moon to three days before new is ideal. Look for features near the *terminator*, the line between lunar night and day. At the terminator, shadows are at their longest and features stand out.

Needless to say, there are too many craters to name here.

But some of the major craters, visible through binoculars, are listed below. (See A Map of the Moon, on pages 28 and 29 for more craters and other features.)

- **Copernicus** (57 miles [93 km] in diameter) One of the most conspicuous craters, visible even to the naked eye, largely because of its bright rays and its isolated position in Oceanus Procellarum. A small telescope will reveal Copernicus's central mountains.
- **Plato** (68 miles [109 km] in diameter) A dark crater on the northern edge of Mare Imbrium.
- **Eratosthenes** (37 miles [59.5 km] in diameter) Not a large crater, but its walls are steep: at least 13,000 feet (about 4,000 m) high. Visible at the southern end of the Apennine Mountains, which are to the northeast of Copernicus.
- **Ptolemaeus** (102 miles [164 km] in diameter), **Alphonsus** (74 miles [119 km] in diameter), and **Arzachel** (60 miles [97 km] in diameter). Three craters in a row just to the east of Mare Nubium. Centered in Alphonsus and Arzachel are small mountains.
- **Tycho** (52 miles [85 km] in diameter) The youngest, at a mere 109 million years of age, and most impressive crater, easily seen by the naked eye during a full Moon, thanks to its spectacular rays. The rays are light-colored impact debris that scattered far and wide, covering older darker material.
- **Longomontanus** (107miles [172 km] in diameter), **Clavius** (140 miles [225 km] in diameter), and **Maginus** (101 miles [163 km] in diameter). Three of the largest craters on the Moon, clumped together near the southern pole, just below Tycho.

Seas on the Moon

A close-up view of Mare Nectaris (center) reveals a smooth plain surrounded by the cratered landscape of the lunar highlands. Hugging the western (left) edge of Nectaris is a trio of large craters: Theophilus (top), Cyrillus, and Catharina. Note the mountains in Theophilus and Cyrillus.

A MAP OF THE MOON

Following is a list of the major Moon features, visible with the naked eye and through binoculars or a small telescope. How many can you observe? Check them off as you find them. Observe them at waning and waxing phases and note changes in their appearances, depending on the way sunlight hits them. Make a note by each feature, indicating whether it's visible with naked eye, binoculars, or a telescope.

CRATERS AND BASINS

- Albategnius
- Alphonsus
- Archimedes
- Aristarchus
- Aristillus
- Aristoteles
- Arzachel
- Catharina
- Clavius
- Copernicus
- Cyrillus
- Eratosthenes
- Gassendi
- Grimaldi
- Kepler
- Longomontanus
- Maginus
- Maurolycus
- Plato
- Ptolemaeus
- Reinhold
- Theophilus
- Tycho

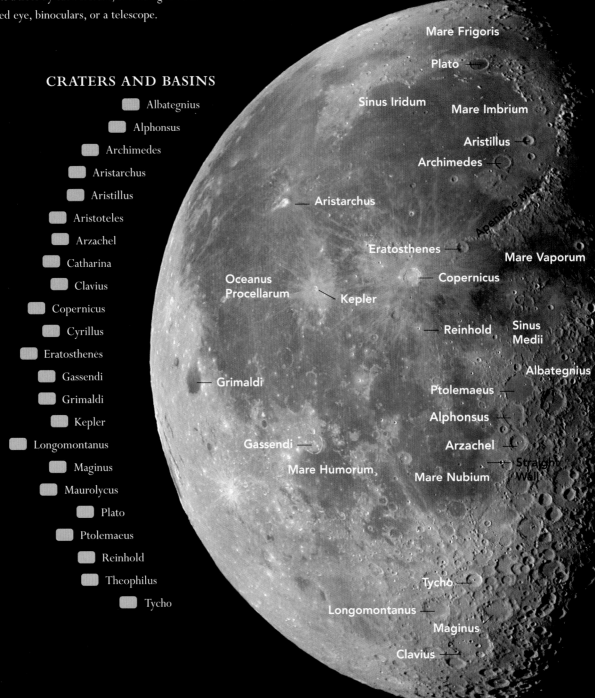

Mare Frigoris
Plato
Aristoteles
Alps Mtns.
Mare Imbrium
Caucasus Mtns.
Archimedes
Mare Serenitatis
Apennine Mtns.
Eratosthenes
Mare
Crisium
Copernicus
Mare Vaporum
Mare Tranquilitatis
Sinus Aestuum
Sinus Medii
Mare
Fecunditatis
Apollo *
Landing
Site
Albategnius
Ptolemaeus
Theophilus
Alphonsus
Cyrillus
Mare
Nectaris
Arzachel
Catharina
Straight
Wall
Mare Nubium
Maurolycus
Tycho
Maginus
Longomontanus
Clavius

MARIA AND OTHER LAVA PLAINS

Mare Crisium (Sea of Crises)

Mare Fecunditatis (Sea of Fertility)

Mare Frigoris (Sea of Cold)

Mare Humorum (Sea of Moisture)

Mare Imbrium (Sea of Rains)

Mare Nectaris (Sea of Nectar)

Mare Nubium (Sea of Clouds)

Mare Serenitatis (Sea of Serenity)

Mare Tranquilitatis

(Sea of Tranquility)

Mare Vaporum (Sea of Vapors)

Sinus Aestuum (Seething Bay)

Sinus Iridum (Bay of Rainbows)

Sinus Medii (Central Bay)

Oceanus Procellarum

(Ocean of Storms)

MOUNTAINS, RILLES
AND FAULTS

Apennine Mtns.

Straight Wall

Caucasus Mtns.

Alps Mtns.

Mountains, rilles, and faults

There aren't many mountain ranges on the earthbound side of the Moon, and they don't resemble Earth's mountains. Lunar mountain ranges are the collapsed rims of the large impact basins that form the maria. You can spot three ranges in the Moon's northern hemisphere, located in a wide arc along the eastern rim of Mare Imbrium: the Alps Mountains at the top, the Caucasus Mountains just below, and to the south, the Apennine Mountains. Other mountains dot the lunar surface, as well, many of them found in the center of larger craters, such as Theophilus, Arzachel, Alphonsus, and Eratosthenes.

Rilles are cracks in the maria, caused by cooling lava as it settled. Possibly the best-known is Hadley Rille, landing site of Apollo 15. Hadley isn't easy to find, but look carefully (you'll need a telescope to see the features listed here) and you may spot three rilles along the eastern edge of Mare Humorum; look three days after first quarter.

Another interesting but tricky-to-spot feature is the Straight Wall in Mare Nubium, near the Arzachel crater. A 75-mile (120-km)-long fault line, the Straight Wall was formed when a section of the mare sank, creating a ridge. Try to catch views of the Straight Wall a day after first quarter or shortly after last quarter—note how its appearance changes from a dark line during the waxing phase to a white line in the waning phase, depending on how the sunlight hits it.

The Moon and Venus
Venus and the crescent Moon make a picturesque pair in the night sky.

NOW YOU SEE IT, NOW YOU DON'T

It's not unusual for the Moon to pass in front of another celestial object, like a planet or a star. When this happens, it's called an *occultation*. In the image at right, the Moon is about to occult the bright star Aldebaran. Because Aldebaran is so far away and is only seen as a pinpoint of light, when the star is occulted, it will simply wink out before it suddenly winks back on again as it emerges on the other side of the Moon. Planets, unlike stars, have discernable disks, so when they're occulted, they will appear, through a telescope, to fade out and then in again.

THE MOON ILLUSION
(IS IT JUST ME, OR IS THAT A REALLY BIG MOON?)

Have you ever watched a summer full Moon as it rises over the horizon? Perhaps it's rising over the edge of a hill or framed by a familiar fringe of trees. As the last rays of the setting sun fade to a copper glow, you take a second look. The Moon seems huge!

Later that evening, you happen to catch sight of that same full Moon, now high in the sky. You glance away, then back. Wait a minute—it's much smaller! How did that happen?

You've just experienced the Moon Illusion, an enigmatic phenomenon that people have been puzzling over for thousands of years. Aristotle was the first to come up with an explanation for it, suggesting that the Earth's atmosphere, acting as a magnifying lens, was the cause of it. In fact, the Earth's atmosphere visually squashes the Moon, which, if anything, should make it appear smaller. Then, in 1,000 AD, an Arabian physicist named Ibn Alhazan suggested that familiar landmarks, such as trees and houses, make the Moon seem large by comparison. After all, we know the Moon is a huge object—it should be enormous, compared to objects on Earth.

Alas, though he came close, Alhazan didn't quite explain it, either, as you still see the effect if you're out in the middle of the ocean with no landmarks at all against which to compare the Moon.

And here's another enigma—if you measure the size of the Moon (with the eraser on the end of a pencil, for example) on the horizon and then high in the sky, you'll discover it's exactly the same size. (Try it—see the Projects section.) Multiple-exposure photographs of the rising Moon also show no change in its size from horizon to zenith. Yet, studies have shown that people estimate the size of the horizon Moon to be as much as twice the size of a zenith Moon.

So, what is going on here? Theories are still being hotly debated. Suffice it to say, what your eyes see and what your brain thinks it's seeing are two different things. It's a purely psychological effect, not a physical one.

Oddly enough, you can dispel the Illusion just by looking at the horizon Moon from a different perspective. If you bend over and look at it from between your legs, the Illusion vanishes. Clearly, it's simply a matter of your point of view.

THE MOON BY NUMBERS

4.5	Age, in billions of years, of the Moon
2,160	Diameter, in miles (3,476 km)
238,800	Average distance from Earth, in miles (384,400 km)
27.3	Number of days to orbit the Earth
27.3	Number of Earth days to rotate once (a lunar day)
29.5	Number of Earth days to complete one lunar cycle (new Moon to new Moon)
109	Age, in millions of years, of Tycho, the Moon's youngest crater
1969	Year Neil Armstrong became the first man to walk on the Moon

PROJECTS

◯ PROJECT 1: Observe the Full Moon

Check your calendar, monthly astronomy magazine, or astronomy website for the date of the next full Moon (your local newspaper will also carry this information). Go outside just after sunset and look in the eastern sky. The Moon will be rising.

Things to do:
- Observe the maria; how many can you name?
- Can you see any craters with the naked eye? How many? Which ones? Tycho is the most obvious crater; can you see its rays? How about the rays around Copernicus? If you're keeping an observing log, you might want to sketch what you see.
- Now take a look at the Moon through binoculars (if you have them). How much more can you see? Check the Map of the Moon and note the features you observe in your observing log.

◯ PROJECT 2: Observe the Phases of the Moon

Check an astronomy website or monthly astronomy magazine to find out what phase the Moon will be in on your observing night and where to look for it. Remember that a new Moon will not be visible, and some phases—generally last quarter to new Moon, the waning phases—are only visible after midnight.

Things to do:
- Observe the Moon's phases with the naked eye over several nights. How many days does it take to notice a change in the phase? Can you identify the phases?
- Observe the crescent Moon. Can you see the Earthshine phenomenon?
- Study the Moon's features over several nights through binoculars. Notice how the features change, according to where the terminator is? You may want to draw them in your observing log. Pick an obvious feature and observe it during the waxing and waning phases (you'll have to stay up late to observe the waning phases); can you see how its appearance changes as the light hits it from different directions? (Note your observations in your log, so you can compare the changes.)

◯ PROJECT 3: Study the Moon Illusion

Check the usual sources to find out when the next Full Moon will occur and where it will rise. Find an unobstructed view of that horizon and note the Moon as it just begins to peek over the horizon. Does it look abnormally large?

Now, measure the horizon Moon with a small disk, something the size of a pencil eraser or a small mint, perhaps—something that just covers it. Try this again later in the evening, when the Moon is higher in the sky. Is the Moon the same size? Does it look smaller than when it was on the horizon?

You can also try looking at the horizon Moon through your legs. Does the Illusion disappear?

○ PROJECT 4: Observing a Lunar Occultation

Check an astronomy website (*http://skyandtelescope.com/observing/ataglance/article_110_1.asp* and *http://www.griffithobs.org/skyreport.html* are two good ones), or use your planetarium software (see Resources, page 150) to find out when the Moon will be near Aldebaran (in Taurus), Regulus (in Leo), Spica (in Virgo), or Antares (in Scorpius). These stars lie in the path of the Moon, which is why it occasionally occults them. On that night, if it's clear, watch with binoculars or a telescope to see whether the Moon occults the star. Observe the star as it "winks" out and then watch to see it reappear on the other side of the Moon. How long does it take before it reappears?

○ PROJECT 5: Observing a Planetary Occultation

Stars aren't the only things to be occulted by the Moon; planets are good occultation subjects, too. Check the Appendix (page 156) for a list of planetary occultations and observe the Moon on those nights. How does a planetary occultation differ from an occultation with a star?

○ PROJECT 6: Watch the Moon Move

You're already familiar with the motion of the Moon around the Earth over the course of a month (it causes the lunar phases), but the Moon moves through the sky during the course of an evening, as well, traveling eastward through the stars by about its own diameter every hour. Check the usual sources to find out when the Moon is in its first-quarter phase—the best time to see this motion is during the few days on either side of it.

Once it's dark, go outside and make a quick sketch that shows the position of the Moon compared to the stars near it. Don't include stars more than three or four lunar diameters away from the Moon. If you can't see any stars that close to the Moon, use binoculars; you should spot a least a couple of faint stars in the same field of view as the lunar orb. (Consider trying this project when the Moon is near Regulus, Spica, Antares, Aldebaran, or Pollux—see above). Then go out again two hours later and compare your sketch to what you see now. You'll discover that the Moon has moved: stars that were once near the left (dark) edge of the Moon are now either closer to that edge or are on the right side of the Moon near its bright limb.

○ PROJECT 7: The Daytime Moon

Check a source to find out when the Moon is in its third-quarter phase and where in the sky it will be. Then head outside early in the morning and see whether you can see the daytime Moon. Can you see any features? Observe it off and on from early morning until it sets at noon and watch its progress across the daytime sky.

CHAPTER THREE
THE PLANETS

When the ancients began observing the heavens, they noticed two things. One was that, although the stars moved across the sky, they seemed to be fixed in place, like diamonds glued to the inside of an indigo sphere that slowly rotated around the Earth. Familiar configurations of stars remained familiar configurations night after night. The Big Dipper, for instance, didn't rise the next night as a teapot.

The second thing they noticed, however, was that five of these "stars" were not fixed in place. They seemed to wander across the sky, first appearing in one constellation, then in another. What was up with that?

They named these renegade stars planets (from the Greek *planetes,* meaning wanderers). Until the late 1700s, those same five—Mercury, Venus, Mars, Jupiter, and Saturn, all visible to the naked eye—were the only ones known. It wasn't until the telescope came into use that the count began to rise. William Herschel was the first to add a planet to the list, with his discovery of Uranus in 1781. Neptune was spotted (by Johann Galle) in 1846 and Pluto (by Clyde Tombaugh) in 1930.

With Pluto in the mix, the solar-system planet count now numbers nine: four terrestrial planets—Mercury, Venus, Earth, and Mars—with rocky cores; four giant planets—Jupiter, Saturn, Uranus, and Neptune—with gaseous compositions; and Pluto, a dim, frozen ball of rock and ice that's in a class all by itself.

Because of their nature as "wanderers," the planets require a little more work to observe than, say, constellations. Their positions change from month to month and year to year. Sometimes, they're closer to Earth; sometimes farther away, depending on where they are in their orbits. Sometimes, they're hidden in the glare of the Sun; and sometimes, they're just too far away to reveal any of their secrets. For these reasons, you'll want to consult the month-by-month charts published in magazines such as *Astronomy, SkyWatch,* and *Night Sky* or found on websites such as *www.astronomy.com* and *www.skyandtelescope.com.* You can also check out one of the available planetarium software programs (see Resources, page 150).

Jupiter is the largest of the solar system's nine planets and one of the most fascinating to observe.

Mercury

Mercury was named for the fleet-footed Roman messenger god—and fleet it is, zipping around the Sun in a speedy eighty-eight days. It's a small world, only about 40 percent larger than the Moon, with about the same appearance, since, like the Moon, Mercury has no atmosphere to speak of, and its surface, battered mercilessly in its youth, has remained unchanged for roughly 3.5 billion years.

In truth, we have never actually seen the entire surface of Mercury. Only one spacecraft has ever visited the planet—Mariner 10, in 1974 and 1975—and it was only able to map about half of it. The Hubble Space Telescope, which has taken amazing photos of the other planets, has never photographed Mercury, either. Why? Because Mercury is just too close to the Sun.

Mercury and Venus

Mercury and Venus, the brighter of the two planets in this photo, punctuate the early morning sky. Mercury's nearness to the Sun makes it a challenging observing subject—and not just for beginning stargazers. Even NASA's space probes haven't captured the whole of it on film. The U.S. space agency has plans to learn more about this least-explored terrestrial planet, however. In August 2004, it launched MESSENGER, a probe that, after performing one Earth, two Venus, and three Mercury flybys, will enter Mercury's orbit in 2011, where it will stay for one year.

Catching even a mere glint of sunlight with Hubble's delicate instruments would severely damage them. Mercury is a challenge to observe from Earth, too—for many reasons. It's a small planet, its proximity to the Sun means most people will never see it in a dark sky, and it's only easily visible for a few weeks each year. Much of the time, Mercury tends to hug the horizon, which can make the planet difficult to find. And when you aim a telescope at it, turbulence in our atmosphere can turn Mercury's disk into a hazy, wobbling blob.

When's the best time to see Mercury? Head outside in the spring or in autumn, when the tilt of the ecliptic is steepest and Mercury is somewhat higher in the sky. This makes it easier to find. In the spring, look for the planet after sunset in the western sky, and in the fall, catch it in the eastern sky about an hour before sunrise. (See the Appendix on page 156 for dates, and check a monthly astronomy magazine or website for exact times; they vary from year to year.)

Observing the planet through a telescope won't be as rewarding as, say, observing the Moon, but you can see Mercury's phases, if the atmospheric turbulence near the horizon isn't too bad. And you'll have the satisfaction of spotting a planet that most people never see at all.

Venus

Venus is often referred to as "Earth's twin," or "sister planet," which is odd, since, other than being close in size, mass, and density, the two planets could not be more dissimilar. Venus is enveloped in a thick, poisonous atmosphere of carbon dioxide and nitrogen, blanketed by layers of sulfuric acid–laced cloud. Its surface pressure is so great (ninety times that of Earth's) that probes sent to explore the planet's surface last no more than several hours before being crushed. Venus's day is longer than

Transit of Venus

Venus and Mercury are called *inferior planets*—their orbits are closer to the Sun than Earth's. (Those planets whose orbits are outside Earth's are called *superior planets*.) Every so often, these two planets' orbits take them in front of the Sun in what's called a *transit*. Here, Venus looks like a small, black disk slowly moving across the face of the Sun—a sort of mini eclipse. Venus last transited the Sun in June 2004, for the first time in 122 years. It will transit again in June 2012, but 105 years will pass before the next one. Mercury transits the Sun on average thirteen times a century. (See Appendix for dates.)

MERCURY BY NUMBERS

3,032	Diameter, in miles (4,879 km)
35,983,095	Average distance from the Sun, in miles (57,909,175 km)
88	Number of Earth days to orbit the Sun
59	Number of Earth days to rotate once
0	Number of moons
−279	Minimum temperature, in degrees Fahrenheit (−173°C)
801	Maximum temperature, in degrees Fahrenheit (427°C)

its year, and its surface temperature, thanks to all that CO_2, is a steamy 864°F (462°C). Underneath the cloud is a landscape of deformed mountain ranges, volcanoes, lava plains, lava domes, and extremely long lava channels (a lot of lava, in other words). Oh, yes—and it has no moon.

The most striking difference? Venus rotates backwards. While Earth (like most planets and the Sun) rotates counter-clockwise, or west to east, Venus rotates clockwise, east to west, or *retrograde*. The Sun rising in Venus's sky (if you could see it through the cloud cover) would rise in the west and set in the east. This is because Venus is essentially upside down, tipped nearly 180° on its axis. Theory has it that the planet may have been hit early on by some huge object with enough force to turn it on its head.

All that sunlight-reflecting cloud cover on Venus, plus its proximity to Earth, makes Venus easy to spot in the night sky. Other than the Moon, Venus is the brightest object up there. In fact, it can be so bright at times that people have mistaken it for a UFO!

Venus isn't always visible in our skies, however. Like all the planets, its orbit takes it out of our field of view for periods of time. During its roughly eighteen-month cycle, you can see it in the western evening sky for about 260 days (between eight and nine months), then, after a gap of a few days, in the eastern morning sky for another eight to nine months. It then disappears from view behind the Sun for two to three months before

beginning the cycle all over again. (See Appendix for dates.)

When Venus *is* in the sky, look for it at dawn or at dusk, up to four hours after sunset or before sunrise. You'll know it when you see it: the planet often referred to as the Morning Star (and Evening Star, in the evening) is usually the first bright object to show up at the celestial party and the last one to leave.

Brilliant as it is to see with the naked eye, Venus is disappointingly featureless when seen through a telescope, although it does present phases, just like Mercury and the Moon.

A Crescent Venus

You'll probably never see Venus in its full phase—when it's near full, it's simply too close to the Sun. Venus in its new phase is never visible, either, unless the planet is transiting the Sun, which happens less than once in a lifetime. This photo of a featureless, cloud-clad, crescent Venus was taken through a 12-inch (300-mm) telescope.

VENUS BY NUMBERS

7,521	Diameter, in miles (12,104 km)
67,237,910	Average distance from the Sun, in miles (108,208,930 km)
225	Number of Earth days to orbit the Sun
243	Number of Earth days to rotate once (retrograde)
0	Number of moons
864	Surface temperature, in degrees Fahrenheit (462°C)

The Ecliptic

From a point in space, just outside the solar system, you can see that Earth and the other planets (except Pluto, because its orbit is tilted) all orbit the Sun in a roughly flat plane, along what is called the *ecliptic*, the path the Sun travels against the background of stars. Seen from Earth, however, this imaginary zone along which the planets move appears tilted in the sky. Why? Because the Earth's axis is tilted. *Planets and orbits not drawn to scale.*

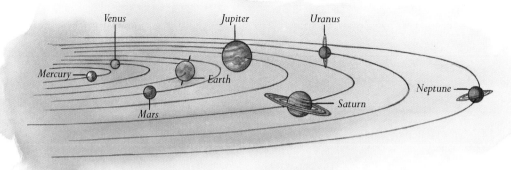

The Ecliptic from Earth

The planets move near a path in the sky known as the ecliptic. Observe the sky when the brighter planets—Venus, Jupiter, and Saturn, for example—are in the sky at the same time. They will all be roughly lined up, often along with the Moon, in an arc across the sky. That arc is where you'll find the ecliptic.

Mars

Has any planet captured our imaginations the way Mars has? The Red Planet has inspired countless novels, movies, and tabloid stories ("The Face on Mars!"), covering topics from terraforming to ancient canal-building civilizations and invasions by little green men. (Oh—and let's not forget *My Favorite Martian*, the popular television series from the Sixties.)

Mars has received a lot of attention from the world's space agencies, as well. As of 2004, thirty-three American, European, Japanese, and Soviet missions—not all of them successful—had been launched to the planet, and more are in the works. Images from the various orbiters, landers, and rovers revealed an arid landscape of rust-red craters, dunes, boulder-strewn plains, massive volcanoes (Olympus Mons, the largest, is fifteen miles, or twenty-four kilometers, high!), and a canyon so vast it sprawls across one-quarter of the planet (Valles Marineris).

Mars has polar ice caps, too, largely made up of frozen carbon-dioxide (aka "dry ice"), mixed with water ice. Because the planet has seasons, the ice caps expand in the winter and shrink in the summer, though the ice doesn't melt so much as evaporate in the thin atmosphere and freezing temperatures. Although no

Mars from Space

NASA's Mars Global Surveyor spacecraft took this shot of the Red Planet. It's late summer in the north and winter in the south, as you can see from the large southern polar ice cap. The dark patch in the center is the volcanic plain Syrtis Major, and the bright area below, near the ice cap, is the Hellas Basin. All are visible at opposition in good-quality backyard telescopes.

liquid water has been discovered on Mars, channels, valleys, and what appear to be dry river beds on the planet's surface make it a fairly certain bet that, at some time in the distant past, at least some regions of Mars were covered in water. Recent probes have also discovered a layer of water ice just below the planet's surface. As for the canals? Just an optical illusion.

Mars isn't called the Red Planet for nothing. Its color, so evident in photos of the planet's surface, is obvious to the naked-eye observer, too. Look along the ecliptic, and, if you see a small, reddish object that isn't twinkling, it's probably Mars.

Observing the planet through binoculars or a telescope can be a bit more challenging. Although Mars (along with Venus and the Moon) is our next-door-neighbor in space, it's still some 35 million miles (56 million km) away from us, at its closest. It's also a small planet—only about half the size of Earth—which is why your first look at it through binoculars or a telescope might be a little disappointing. The view improves when Mars is at *opposition* (see illustration on page 41), when its nearness turns it from a tiny, fuzzy, orange ball tipped with white to a larger, fuzzy, orange ball dappled by areas of dark and light. You'll need at least

Mars at Opposition

A bright Mars hangs in the sky over the Boston skyline. In this photo, Mars is at opposition; that is, when it is closest to Earth—roughly every two years—and its brightness is rivaled only by Venus's. As the planet's orbit takes it farther from Earth, it appears considerably dimmer and smaller, and its features become harder to detect.

Volcanoes and Canyons

Clouds of water ice crystals hover over the peaks of four enormous volcanoes—Olympus Mons, Ascraeus Mons, Pavonis Mons, and Arsia Mons—on Mars's Tharsis plain in this photo taken by NASA's Mars Global Surveyor. A dust storm swirls across the top right portion of the planet, and at the center is a large gash—the 3,000-mile (5,000-km)-long Valles Marineris. Huge dust storms regularly rage across the surface of Mars, sometimes obscuring all detail from view.

Mars from Earth

If you've seen photos of Mars at all, they've probably been from one of the many spacecraft that have visited the planet. This photo, taken through a 14-inch (350-mm) telescope, represents what you're more likely to see from an Earth-based backyard scope (albeit a large one).

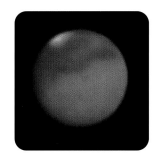

a 3-inch (75-mm) telescope to see any of Mars's features. (Astronomy magazines usually publish a map showing Martian features several months before opposition.)

Don't be discouraged; it takes patience, practice—and steady air—to see anything resembling detail on Mars's surface. But, once you become familiar with what you're looking at, Mars through the telescope can be a fascinating subject. And you can get to know its features in a relatively short time, thanks to the planet's rotational period, which is only thirty-seven minutes longer than Earth's. This means that, over the course of an evening, Mars rotates enough to bring new features into view. Observe Mars at the same time each evening, and, in a little more than a month, you'll have seen the entire planet. (Or, if you're up for an eight-hour Mars observing marathon, about one-third of it.) What you may never see, however, especially through a smaller telescope, are Mars's moons, Phobos and Deimos. The tiny, oddball-shaped, orbiting chunks of rock are thought to be objects captured from the asteroid belt by Mars's gravity.

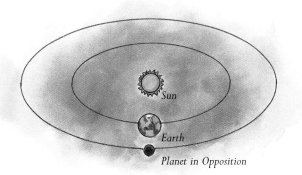

Planet in Opposition

Opposition

Superior planets—those planets whose orbits are larger than Earth's—are best viewed when they are at *opposition;* that is, when they're directly opposite the Sun and closest to Earth.

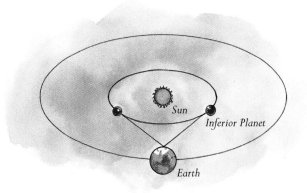

Inferior Planet

Earth

Elongation

Inferior planets—whose orbits lie between the Earth and the Sun: Mercury and Venus—are best observed when they're near *greatest elongation;* that is, when they're at their greatest angular separation east or west of the Sun.

MARS BY NUMBERS

4,222	Diameter, in miles (6,794 km)
141,633,260	Average distance from the Sun, in miles (227,936,640 km)
687	Earth days to orbit the Sun
24.6	Earth hours to rotate once
2	Number of moons
−125	Minimum surface temperature, in degrees Fahrenheit (−87°C)
	(although winter lows at the poles can plunge below −148°F/−100°C)
23	Maximum surface temperature, in degrees Fahrenheit (−5°C)

Jupiter

Behemoth of the solar system, grand-daddy of all planets, Jupiter is so large that eleven Earths could fit across its diameter and some 1,300 could fit inside it. The planet and its moons are like a miniature solar system within a solar system—as of 2004, *sixty-three* moons had been discovered circling the great, belted giant. (Check out *www.skyandtelescope.com/observing/objects/planets* for a current count of Jupiter's moons.)

Those dark belts and bright zones are layers of cloud, swirling in opposite directions, as the planet—or most of it, anyway—whirls about on its axis at an alarmingly swift nine hours and fifty-five minutes. Jupiter's equatorial region, however, actually rotates five minutes *faster* than the rest of the planet, which creates all sort of turbulence at the boundaries between the belts and zones. The most well-known area of turbulence is the Great Red Spot (although it has, over the years, come to look more like a great pink or pale-orange spot), an enormous storm twice the width of Earth that has been raging for hundreds of years.

Underneath those swirling gas clouds? More gas, mostly hydrogen and helium. Jupiter, like all the "gas giants," has no solid surface. Scientists believe that, deep inside the planet, the

Eye to Io
Jupiter and its moon, Io, stare each other down in this photo taken by NASA's Cassini spacecraft. Note the Great Red Spot amid the giant planet's swirling cloud belts.

gas gets compressed into liquid hydrogen; at its center may be a core of molten rock. In fact, in composition, Jupiter is very much like our Sun; had the planet been fifty to one hundred times more massive, it would have become a dim star, rather than a planet. (See Chapter Five for more on what makes a star.)

Jupiter's enormous size and reflective clouds make it the second-brightest planet in the night sky. Only Venus is brighter. Visible ten months of the year, Jupiter will sometimes appear with Saturn, Venus, and a paler Mars, aligned along the ecliptic in what's called a conjunction.

What you probably can't see with the naked eye are any of Jupiter's moons. It was Galileo who first discovered the planet's four largest moons through his telescope, which is why they're often referred to as Galilean satellites. Thanks to today's improved optics, you need only a good pair of steadily held binoculars to see Io, Europa, Ganymede, and Callisto. Observe

Jupiter and Moons from Earth
Jupiter with its moons, (left to right) Ganymede, Europa, Callisto, and Io, as they would appear through a small telescope.

Jupiter's Moons— Close up
This composite image of Jupiter's four largest moons, taken by NASA's Galileo orbiter, includes (left to right, shown in scale and in order of increasing distance from Jupiter) Io, Europa, Ganymede, and Callisto.

Planets Over the City Skyline

Venus and Jupiter in the evening sky in February 1999, before coming to conjunction. Although Jupiter is a much larger planet, Venus, at lower right, is the brighter of the two, because of its proximity to Earth and its reflective clouds. Jupiter, however, is usually the second-brightest planet.

them over the course of a few nights and you'll see them change positions: now lined up on one side of the planet; now paired on either side; sometimes at varying distances from Jupiter and each other; sometimes disappearing behind or in front of the planet's bright disk.

A small (3- to 5-inch [75- to 125-mm]) telescope will bring Jupiter's two major belts and—when the air is steady—the Great Red Spot into view, while a larger (8-inch [200-mm]) scope will reveal fainter belts and, possibly, even the looping patterns called *festoons*, areas where darker belt material is swept up into the lighter zones. Because of the speed of Jupiter's rotation, the view changes noticeably in just a few hours, making it one of the most fascinating celestial objects to observe.

JUPITER BY NUMBERS

88,846	Diameter, in miles (142,984 km)
483,682,810	Average distance from the Sun, in miles (778,412,020 km)
11.6	Earth years to orbit the Sun
9.9	Earth hours to rotate once
63+	Number of moons
−234	Cloud-top temperature, in degrees Fahrenheit (−148°C)

Saturn

If ever there was a jewel in our necklace of planets, it's Saturn. Few people will forget their first view of the planet and its rings through a telescope. It looks pretty good in those NASA photos, too—as planets go, Saturn's a hottie, all right.

While all four of the giant planets have rings, Saturn's win the prize for most spectacular. Up close, they're myriad ringlets made up of billions of icy, dust- to house-sized particles, circling the cream-colored orb of Saturn in a sheet 169,600 miles (273,000 km) across but only tens to hundreds of yards (meters) thick. The rings vary in brightness and are separated by gaps that seem empty but are really just areas with fewer particles. The largest gap, the Cassini division, is wide enough to hold most of the planet Mercury.

Circling outside the rings, like watchful parents at the playground, are most of Saturn's myriad moons (thirty-four, as of 2004). A very few—called shepherd moons— travel among the rings, ensuring the particles orbit the planet in an orderly fashion and don't wander off into space. Of Saturn's five largest moons, Titan, as its name suggests, is the biggest; it's the second-largest moon in the solar system and is larger even than Mercury and Pluto. You can easily spot Titan through a small telescope, but you'll need a 6-inch (150-mm), or larger, scope to see Saturn's four other major moons.

Saturn is huge (only Jupiter beats it for size), but it's nearly twice as distant as Jupiter—to the naked eye, Saturn looks like a bright star. Binoculars won't do much to improve the view, and you'll need a telescope to see the awe-inspiring rings. The good news is that even a small telescope will show them. The not-so-good news? The rings won't be nearly as resplendent as those depicted in the NASA photos. You can increase the "awe quotient" by visiting your local planetarium or observatory on a public viewing night and observing Saturn through a large scope. That first look at Saturn and its bracelet of pale-gold rings will raise goosebumps!

Ringed Majesty

NASA's Cassini space probe, which went into orbit around Saturn on July 1, 2004, took this photo of the planet and its resplendent rings. Like Jupiter, Saturn is a gas planet, composed mainly of hydrogen and helium, and its atmosphere is turbulent, with extreme super-hurricane-force winds blasting across the upper atmosphere. Like Jupiter, it has belts and zones. Unlike Jupiter, its features are harder to see, due to a layer of haze above the main cloud decks.

A Scope View of Saturn

Saturn, as seen through a 5-inch (125-mm) telescope, reveals its rings, along with the gap known as the Cassini division. Barely visible are Saturn's belts. In this photo, the tilt of Saturn and its rings provides a good view of both (you may even be able to make out the planet's shadow against the rings). At times during Saturn's orbit around the Sun, however, the planet's rings are edge-on and are barely visible at all.

SATURN BY NUMBERS

74,898	Diameter, in miles (120,536 km)
885,904,700	Average distance from the Sun, in miles (1,426,725,400 km)
29.4	Earth years to orbit the Sun
10.6	Earth hours to rotate once
34+	Number of moons
–288	Cloud-top temperature, in degrees Fahrenheit (–178°C)

Tilting at the Sun

Like Earth and all the planets, to varying degrees, Saturn is tilted on its axis (27°). As the planet travels along its twenty-nine-year orbit, first one hemisphere, then the other is tipped toward the Sun. This cyclical change causes seasons on Saturn, just as Earth's tilt causes seasons on our planet. These Hubble Space Telescope images, taken from 1996 to 2000, show Saturn's rings opening up from just past edge-on to nearly fully open, as the planet moves from spring toward summer in its southern hemisphere.

The Outer Planets

Latecomers to the solar system party, because of their remoteness in space, Uranus (and let's clear up the pronunciation thing: it's YUR-uh-nus, not yer-AY-nus), Neptune, and Pluto were only discovered once the telescope was invented. No wonder. Uranus is just barely visible to the naked eye (under very dark skies), and binoculars are needed to see Neptune—as long as you know where to look. As for Pluto, well, you'll need at least an 8-inch (200-mm) scope, dark skies, and a good deal of patience, practice, and experience to see anything of this tiny planet. Even the Hubble Space Telescope isn't able to produce a decent photo of Pluto—the planet is just too small and too far away to be anything but a mystery to most of us. It will take a closer look by future space probes to shed more light on Pluto.

Uranus and Neptune are part of the family of giant planets, similar in composition to Jupiter

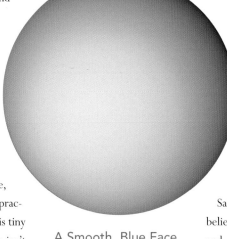

A Smooth, Blue Face

Methane in Uranus's upper atmosphere gives the planet its blue hue. Unlike the other gas giants, Uranus has no colorful bands or great storms, though recent photos have shown clouds on its face. This image was taken by NASA's Voyager 2 spacecraft in 1986.

and Saturn. Like the other gas giants, Uranus and Neptune spin rapidly—Uranus rotating in seventeen hours, fourteen minutes, and Neptune in just sixteen hours, seven minutes. They also have faint ring systems. They differ, however, in a number of ways—size, for one thing. Uranus and Neptune, similar in size to each other, are about half the size of Saturn and roughly twice as dense. (In fact, given a large enough body of water, Saturn would float!) Some astronomers believe the relatively high densities of Uranus and Neptune indicate they have large, solid cores of rock and ice, plus significant amounts of water. Their color sets them apart, as well. Methane in their atmospheres gives them a blue to blue-green hue, with Uranus presenting a smooth, discreetly clouded face and Neptune showing only a few features, one of which was a storm not unlike Jupiter's Great

Pluto and Charon

So distant, dim, and small is Pluto that even the Hubble Space Telescope has difficulty getting a good shot of the tiny planet and its moon, Charon (right). This image was taken when the planet was 2.6 billion miles (4.4 billion km) from Earth.

Red Spot. Called the Great Dark Spot, it disappeared sometime between its discovery by Voyager 2 in 1989 and later observations by the Hubble Space Telescope in 1994.

Where Uranus departs radically from Neptune, the gas giants, and every other planet in the solar system is in its axis: it's tilted 98°, as if some huge, bullying space object had come along and, just for laughs, tipped it over on its side. Indeed, that's what astronomers think happened (well, more or less).

Uranus and Neptune each have an extensive collection of moons: twenty-seven for Uranus and thirteen for Neptune (as of 2004). You're not likely to see any of them, however, without a large telescope and plenty of experience. Uranus can be seen as a small, greenish disk in a small telescope, but even a large one won't show Neptune as much more than a pale, bluish dot. Don't be disappointed, though; remember that

The Late, Great Dark Spot

Like Uranus, Neptune gets its blue color from an abundance of methane in its upper atmosphere. In this photo, taken by NASA's Voyager 2 spacecraft in 1989, Neptune's Great Dark Spot, a huge storm, similar to Jupiter's Great Red Spot, is clearly visible. Sometime after Voyager's flyby, however, the Dark Spot disappeared—photos taken by the Hubble Telescope in early 2004 showed a "spotless" Neptune.

you're looking at objects that are billions of miles away—no mean feat!

Even further away than Uranus and Neptune, circling in its own eccentric orbit around the Sun once every 248 years, is Pluto, with its one known moon, Charon. A tiny ball of rock and ice, Pluto belongs to neither the gaseous nor the terrestrial families of planets. In fact, some astronomers question whether it should be considered a planet at all. In size and composition, Pluto is more like the icy worlds that inhabit the Kuiper Belt, and its odd orbit lends credence to the theory that the tiny, frozen world is really a large Kuiper Belt object captured by the pull of the Sun's gravity. As astronomers discover more objects on the outer fringes of our solar system, the question of "what makes a planet" continues to be debated.

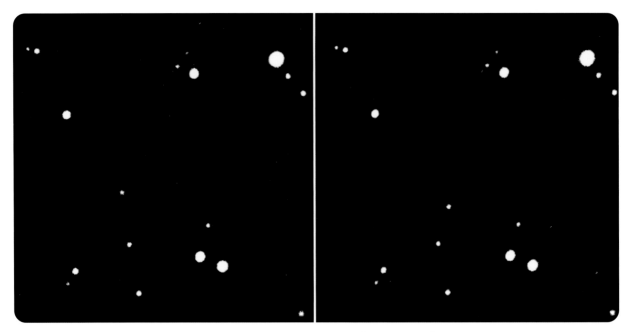

Spot the Asteroid

Identical photographs of a starfield? Not quite. Astronomer Dennis di Cicco took this pair of images, both of which contain an asteroid. Look carefully at the third dot up from the bottom left in the left-hand photo, then find that dot in the photo on the right. You'll notice that it has moved. The dot is the asteroid.

The Asteroid Belt

Some 342,000,000 miles (roughly 550,000,000 km) of space separate Mars and Jupiter. Although we know it's not empty, it certainly appeared that way to pre-nineteenth-century astronomers. They had their doubts, though: the planets in the solar system seemed to be arranged in too orderly a fashion for such a large gap to be without *something* in it. There had to be a planet there; they just hadn't found it yet. So convinced were they that, for years, a group of German astronomers searched in vain for the missing orb.

It wasn't until January 1801 that an Italian astronomer named Giovanni Piazzi discovered an object orbiting in the seemingly empty space. It was an asteroid. Named Ceres (since Greek mythology was still a popular well from which celestial names were being drawn), it was soon followed by another asteroid discovery—Pallas—and later Juno and Vesta.

What's an asteroid? It's a chunk of rock in orbit around the Sun between Mars and Jupiter. Roughly 22,000, of an estimated *one billion* asteroids orbiting in the Asteroid Belt, have been observed since Piazzi's discovery. (Contrary to what science-fiction films will tell you, however, the asteroids are not jammed cheek-by-jowl in the Belt; in fact, they're typically separated by several million miles—which is a good thing, or probes such as Galileo and Cassini, en route to Jupiter and Saturn, would be in a whole lot of trouble.) About one million of those have a diameter of about two-thirds of a mile (one km) or more; none are more than 620 miles (1,000 km) across.

Why are the asteroids there? Two theories have been proposed: one is that a small planet once existed there but was smashed to smithereens by some passing object; the other, which has come to be the generally accepted theory, is that a planet was supposed to have formed from the debris but didn't quite come together.

Asteroids are tricky to find, but you can see them. Vesta is visible to the naked eye—on occasion and under a very dark sky—and Ceres, Pallas, and Juno are bright enough to be easily seen through binoculars. To learn more about observing asteroids, see the websites listed in the Resources section, page 150.

NEAR-EARTH OBJECTS

In 1989, an object about 218 yards (200 m) in diameter passed within 497,000 miles (800,000 km) of Earth. Another, smaller object passed by just 65,243 miles (105,000 km) from us in 1994. More recently, Asteroid Toutatis, which visited in 1992, dropped by for a return visit. We call these invaders of Earth's personal space *Near-Earth Objects*, or NEOs.

Collisions between Earth and solar system debris have happened before in our planet's geological history; they will happen again. But there's no point in worrying about it. (It's like living near a dormant volcano: you know it could erupt someday, but you don't know when, and there isn't much you can do about it, anyway.) If you do want to find out more about these rogue asteroids, check out NASA/JPL's NEO website, (see Resources, page 150).

URANUS BY NUMBERS

31,764	Diameter, in miles (51,118 km)
1,783,939,400	Average distance from the Sun, in miles (2,870,972,200 km)
84	Earth years to orbit the Sun
17.24	Earth hours to rotate once (retrograde)
27+	Number of moons
−357	Cloud-top temperature, in degrees Fahrenheit (−216°C)

NEPTUNE BY NUMBERS

30,776	Diameter, in miles (49,528 km)
2,795,084,800	Average distance from the Sun, in miles (4,498,252,900 km)
165	Earth years to orbit the Sun
16.1	Earth hours to rotate once
13	Number of moons
−353	Cloud-top temperature, in degrees Fahrenheit (−214°C)

PLUTO BY NUMBERS

1,430	Diameter, in miles (2,302 km)
3,670,050,000	Average distance from the Sun, in miles (5,906,380,000 km)
248	Earth years to orbit the Sun
6.4	Earth days to rotate once
1	Number of moons
−387	Minimum surface temperature, in degrees Fahrenheit (−233°C)
−369	Maximum surface temperature, in degrees Fahrenheit (−223°C)

PROJECTS

○ PROJECT 1: Find the Ecliptic

Check an astronomy website or monthly astronomy magazine to find out what planets will be visible in the sky and when. You'll also want to check their location. Try to go out on a night when a few planets—Mars, Jupiter, and Saturn, for instance—are up at around the same time. Once you've spotted them, note their positions in the sky. Are they lined up roughly in an arc? If the Moon is out, note whether it is lined up roughly in the same arc. If so, you've found the path of the ecliptic. Note where it is in relation to your horizon, then go out at about the same time of night at different seasons, to see whether the ecliptic is higher or lower in the sky.

○ PROJECT 2: Observing Venus

Flip ahead to the Appendix (page 156), to see whether Venus will be visible. Look for it in the western sky, in the evening, just after sunset. Observe Venus through binoculars. Can you see any color? Does it resolve itself into a disk? If you have a small telescope, observe Venus at low power. Can you see determine its phase? Observe it over a few weeks. Can you see the changes in phase? Observe Venus through binoculars and/or a telescope when it's near the horizon and then again when Venus is a little higher in the sky. Does the view of Venus improve when it is higher above the horizon?

○ PROJECT 3: Observing Mercury

Follow the same steps for finding Venus to locate Mercury. Can you find it? Mercury can be easier to spot when the crescent Moon is nearby. If not, be patient. Some people never see Mercury at all. When you do spot it, observe it through binoculars. What can you see? Follow the steps for Venus to observe Mercury through a small telescope.

○ PROJECT 4: Watch Mars Move

Check a website or monthly astronomy magazine or use planetarium software to find out when Mars will be visible in the evening sky. Note Mars's position against the background of stars. Which constellation is it in? You might want to make a simple sketch in your observing log that shows the position of Mars relative to some nearby stars. Don't include where it is in relation to the horizon; just note its position among the stars. (You could also photocopy a star map and mark the planet's positions on it.) Two weeks later, find Mars again, and record its location. Has it moved? Observe Mars regularly over the course of several months, noting the constellations through which it moves. Does it seem to move faster or slower at times? Observe the planet's movement as it nears opposition (see Appendix [page 156] for dates). Does its movement slow down? Even stop? What happens when it's past opposition? Does it seem to speed up again?

○ PROJECT 5: Observe Mars's Brightness

Observe Mars periodically, from about four months before opposition (see Appendix [page 156] for dates) and observe any changes in the planet's brightness before and after opposition.

○ PROJECT 6: Observing Mars through a Telescope

Observe Mars periodically, from about two months before opposition (see Appendix for dates). Note the increase in size of the planet and the amount of visible detail as it nears opposition. Note when they start to diminish again. What can you see at opposition? Polar caps? Dark areas? Brighter areas? Can you identify them? Observe nightly, at the same time of evening, to see changes in Mars's features. Go out forty minutes later each evening, to study the same area on Mars's globe. By observing over a few hours, you will see more features, as the planet rotates.

○ PROJECT 7: Observe Jupiter through Binoculars

Check an astronomy magazine or website to find out when Jupiter will be visible in the evening sky. Through binoculars, observe Jupiter's moons. How many can you see? Note their positions in your observing log. Watch over several nights and note how their positions change.

○ PROJECT 8: Observe Jupiter through a Telescope

Can you see the cloud belts? How many can you see? Draw Jupiter in your observing log. Can you see the Red Spot? Watch the Spot over several nights, and observe its movement. Is it brighter or fainter at times? Draw its position in your observing log.

○ PROJECT 9: Observe Saturn through a Telescope

Check an astronomy magazine or website to find out when Saturn will be visible in the evening sky. Observe the rings. Can you see the Cassini division? Look for Titan and other visible moons, and observe any changes in their positions. Note, too, the tilt of the rings, and draw them in your observing log. A long-term project is to watch how, over a period of years, the tilt of Saturn's rings changes. On September 4, 2009, Saturn's rings will be edge-on to Earth, and for roughly a month before and after this date, the planet will appear ringless.

○ PROJECT 10: Find Uranus and Neptune

Check an astronomy magazine or website to find out when Uranus and Neptune will be visible in the evening sky. You might also want to check a detailed sky atlas for help in finding their positions. Then try to find the distant planets, first with binoculars, then with a telescope. They may take some time to spot.

○ PROJECT 11: Find an asteroid

This project, like number 10, is a little challenging for beginner stargazers but all the more rewarding when you meet with success. After all, how many people have seen an asteroid? You'll need to refer to an astronomy magazine or website to find out when Ceres, Juno, Pallas, and Vesta are visible and where to look for them. When you find one, track it over a few evenings, then go on to the next one. See whether you can "bag" all four of them. Of course, you don't have to stop with the four bright asteroids. There are plenty of fainter ones to observe, too, if you want even more of a challenge.

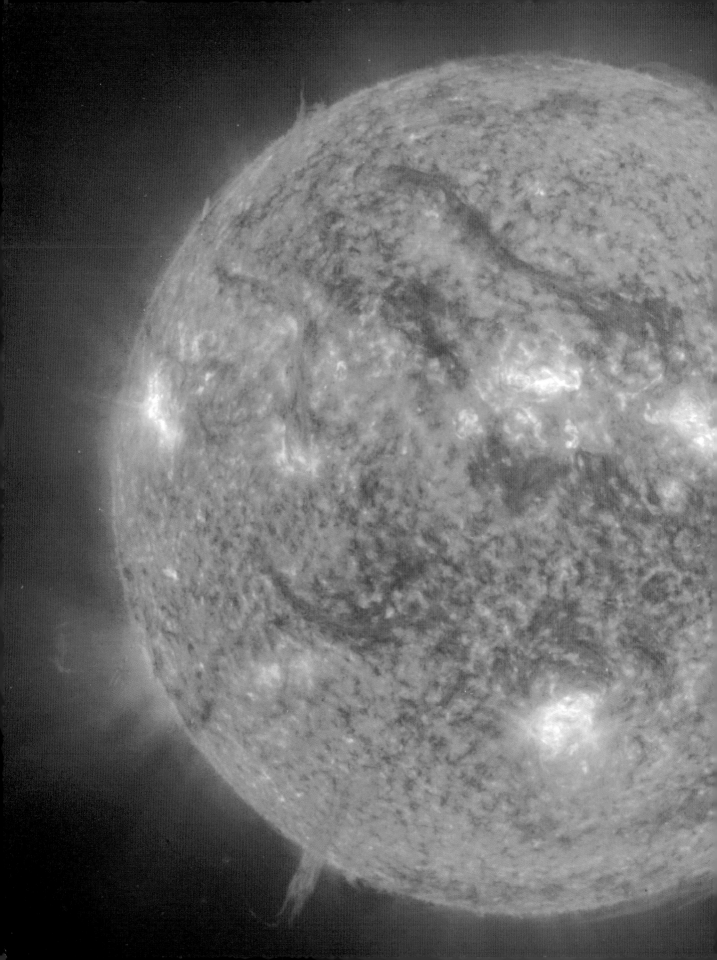

CHAPTER FOUR
THE SUN

It's been called a lot of things—Ra by the Egyptians, Helios and Apollo by the Greeks, Sol by the Romans—but we know it as the Sun. Worshipped for centuries by many ancient cultures, the Sun was revered for its role as the giver of life.

Times change, however, and the Sun is pretty much taken for granted, these days, unless it's being eclipsed by the Moon or transited by Mercury or Venus. The ancients did have it right, though—nothing is more important to our continued existence than the Sun. Why? Because the Sun is our sole source of heat and light. And without it, we'd be in a lot of trouble.

First, a Little Background

Our Sun is a star, just one of countless billions shining in the black void of space. A seething ball of mostly hydrogen gas, it was born about 4.6 billion years ago out of a swirling mass of interstellar gas and dust. (What didn't become the Sun—less than one tenth of 1 percent—became the rest of the solar system.) Although it's been described as medium-small on the stellar size scale, in relation to the rest of our solar system, it's immense. If you were to make a model of the solar system, you'd need a basketball for the Sun and a pinhead to represent the Earth!

Solar Turbulence
An enormous, handle-shaped prominence erupts from the surface of the Sun in this photo taken in ultra-violet light by the SOHO spacecraft in 1999.

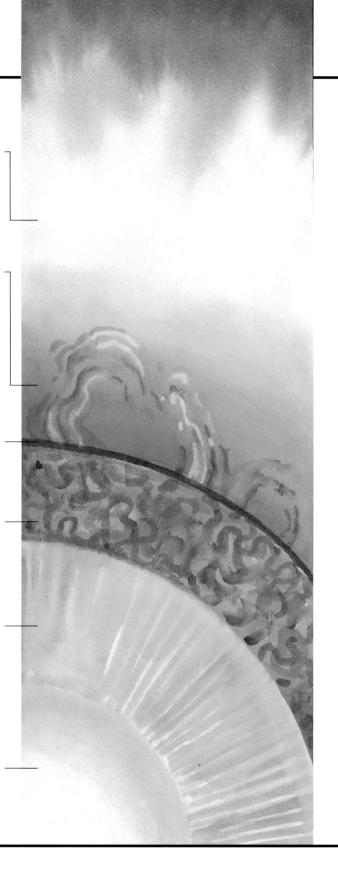

Corona

Invisible, except during a total solar eclipse, when you can see it with the naked eye, the corona is a white-hot veil of rarified gas stretching into space. Temperatures in the outermost layer of the Sun's atmosphere exceed 2 million degrees Fahrenheit (about 1 million degrees Celsius).

Chromosphere

Home of solar flares and prominences. To this point, the temperature in each successive layer of the Sun, from the core to the photosphere, has dropped. But in the chromosphere, the layer above the Sun's surface, the temperature suddenly leaps to 18,000°F (10,000°C) from 9,900°F (5,500°C). Scientists still haven't figured out why this happens, but it's been a mystery for some time.

Photosphere

The photosphere is what's referred to when we speak of the Sun's "surface." This is the layer housing sunspots.

Convection Layer

The convection layer is much like a simmering pot of thick soup; bubbles of hot gas rise to the surface, then sink as they cool and are replaced by more hot bubbles.

Radiation Layer

Gamma rays produced in the core bounce around in the radiation layer for hundreds of thousands of years before working their way to the surface of the Sun and escaping into space.

Core

The core is where nuclear fusion takes place, the process that makes the Sun shine and provides heat and light to Earth. Unlike Earth's, the Sun's core is not solid—it's hot, dense gas.

More than 1.3 million planets the size of ours would fit inside our local star.

The Sun is also hot—a raging furnace of thermonuclear fusion. Deep down at the Sun's core, where the temperature is 29 million degrees Fahrenheit (16 million degrees Celsius), hydrogen is being transformed into helium, the process releasing enormous amounts of energy—equivalent to detonating roughly ninety billion one-megaton nuclear bombs every second. That energy works its way slowly, over hundreds of thousands of years, through to the Sun's surface, where it is radiated out into space as light and heat. Eight minutes from the time it leaves the Sun, it's welcomed by a crowd of sunbathers on Earth.

With the exception, perhaps, of science-fiction writers and those people who stand on street corners with signs declaring, "The End is Near," most of us don't think much about whether or not the Sun will rise tomorrow. After all, it's been around for 4.6 billion years, hasn't it? But what happens down the road? The lifespan of a star the size and mass of the Sun is about ten billion years, which means it still has at least five billion to shine before the interstellar Grim Reaper arrives. During its senior years, as the hydrogen fuel at the core runs out and its hydrogen shell begins to burn, the Sun will begin to swell up and become a giant red ball, releasing its outer layers into the solar system and turning the Earth into a dried-out, scorched husk of its former self. What's left, once the Sun's outer layers eventually drift away, will be a small, white-dwarf star. (See more about stars and their lifecycles in the next chapter.)

Observing the Sun—Safely

The Sun is a fascinating subject to observe. It's a chance to watch a star up close! Unlike many stars in the night sky, it's bright, easy to find—and you don't have to stay up all night to see it.

The downside? **You can seriously damage your eyes if you don't observe safely! Never, *ever* look directly at the Sun**—not with your naked eyes and especially not through unfiltered binoculars or a telescope! The lenses and mirrors in them act just like a magnifying glass, concentrating the light into a laserlike beam that can burn your retinas and cause permanent blindness.

So, how can you safely observe the Sun? By using one of two methods: projection viewing or solar filters.

Projection Viewing

Projection viewing allows a concentrated beam of light to pass through the telescope onto white cardstock held in front of the eyepiece. Small telescopes are better for projection viewing—the heat generated by the light can damage larger scopes.

Projection Viewing This is the low-tech, low-cost way to observe the Sun, your only investment a piece of white cardstock. However, you should use projection viewing only if you have a simple telescope, such as a refractor (which uses a lens) or a Newtonian reflector (which uses a mirror). More complex scopes like catadioptrics (Schmidt- or Maksutov-Cassegrains), which use a combination of lenses and mirrors, can be damaged by the intense heat generated by the solar image. If you own a catadioptric telescope, use a solar filter, instead. (For more about telescopes, see Chapter Ten.)

For projection viewing, mount your scope on a tripod and install a low-power eyepiece (use the lowest you have). Cover the finder, or take it off altogether. *Without sighting through or along the tube,* aim the telescope in the direction of the Sun, adjusting the scope's angle as you check its shadow on the ground. When you have the smallest shadow possible, and sunlight is coming through the eyepiece, you're aligned. Now, hold a piece of white cardstock in front of the eyepiece and adjust its position until you see a sharp image of the Sun on the card. You may need to fix a second card around the tube if there's too much glare on the card to see the image properly.

You still need to practice caution when viewing by projection. The beam of light coming out of the eyepiece is like a laser beam—it can seriously burn you, so be careful not to inadvertently put your hand—or any other part of your body—between the eyepiece and the card. Take extra care if children are around, and never leave the scope unattended. All it takes is an accidental bump and someone could be easily hurt.

Solar projection works best with small telescopes (up to four inches [100 mm]). If you have a larger scope and want to view by projection, cut a small, circular hole in a piece of cardboard and tape it over the front end of the tube, to reduce the amount of light and heat entering the scope.

Solar Filters

Solar filters are a better choice for larger telescopes, which can be damaged by intense heat from the solar image. They fit over the front end of the scope and block most of the incoming light. Solar filters come in many standard sizes, for telescopes as well as binoculars. Glass filters are more expensive than polymer-film filters, but they're also more durable. You can also buy sheets of polymer film and make your own solar filters; the sheets come with instructions. (See Resources for sources.)

Solar Filters Made of metal-coated optical glass or polymer film, solar filters fit over the front end of your telescope. They work by blocking most of the light entering the tube. Glass filters show the Sun in white light, while polymer-film filters give the Sun a blue tint. If money is no object, you may want to invest in an H-alpha (hydrogen-alpha) filter. These high-end filters (costing upwards of $1,000) reveal the Sun in glorious detail and are the only filters that will show prominences.

Avoid filters that screw into the eyepiece end of the telescope. These allow a concentrated beam of light to pass through the telescope tube, until being blocked at the eyepiece. The intense heat from that concentrated beam can damage your scope and cause these filters to suddenly crack or separate, letting the light hit your eye. And just a little exposure goes a long way toward permanent eye damage.

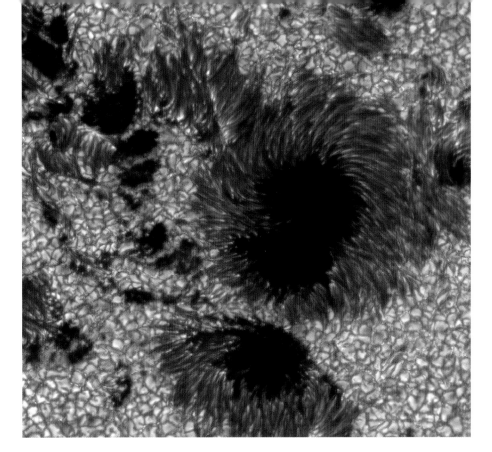

Solar Acne

They may look like stains on your shag carpeting, but these are sunspots up close—very close. Sunspots are cooler areas on the Sun and usually appear in pairs or groups. They vary greatly in size; the largest ones, which can span the width of the Earth several times, are sometimes visible to the unaided eye (using a filter). The dark area in the center of the sunspot is called the umbra. It's surrounded by the penumbra, which is lighter—and slightly hotter—than the umbra. This photo was taken with the Swedish 1-Meter Solar Telescope (SST) from the Canary Islands.

Naked-Eye and Binocular Viewing What if you don't have a telescope? Can you still observe the Sun? Yes. Naked-eye viewing is easy and inexpensive. Just go down to your local hardware or welder's supply store (you may have to check the Yellow Pages) and ask for a number 13 or 14 welder's plate. It's large enough to cover both your eyes when you hold it up between them and the Sun and will block enough light for a safe view. Special goggles and glasses made from polymer film are also available from some telescope manufacturers (see Resources). Just be sure the lenses don't have scratches or holes in them.

As for binoculars, the same welder's plate can be taped securely over the lens end of them. You can also buy both coated-glass and polymer-film solar filters, sized to fit binoculars. If you'd rather do projection viewing, mount the binoculars on a tripod and cap one of the lenses. Then follow the same procedure as for telescope projection viewing.

Use these safe-viewing practices every time you observe the Sun, even during events like solar eclipses and transits.

What Can You See?

Sunspots They look like freckles or blemishes on the Sun, and they usually occur in pairs or small groups. If you observe the Sun over a few days, you'll see that they move from east to west, as the Sun rotates. They will also change in number, appearing and disappearing in a matter of days or weeks, although a few may last for months. Sunspots follow an eleven-year cycle; that is, they seem to peak in number (called a solar maximum) roughly every eleven years. Between peaks, the numbers dwindle, to a point where very few sunspots are visible (the solar minimum). The number of sunspots at each solar maximum can vary from one cycle to the next. Some years, the Sun looks like it has a bad case of acne; in others, peak numbers can look positively anemic. (Sometimes, decades will go by with very little sunspot activity, such as the stretch from 1645 to 1715, called the Maunder Minimum, when very few sunspots were visible.) The most recent solar maximum was in 2000, so, with any luck, another good crop will arise as we approach 2011. While an abundance of sunspots makes for fascinating viewing—and spectacular auroral displays—all that

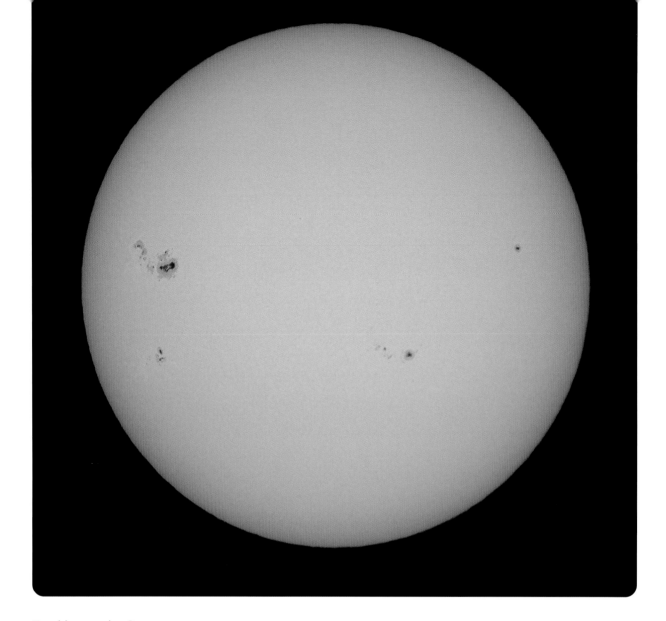

Freckles on the Sun

Sunspots mark the face of the Sun in this photo, taken through a 4-inch (100-mm) refractor equipped with a coated-glass solar filter. The largest of these sunspots was visible with the naked eye (through a solar filter). Although the solar disk appears smooth, it's anything but; hot gas constantly bubbles to the surface, forming granular cels as large as 600 miles (about 1,000 km) across, while in the sunspot areas, massive magnetic fields burst through the photosphere and extend thousands of miles into space.

THE SUN BY NUMBERS

93,000,000	Miles between Earth and the Sun (149,598,000 km)
864,500	Diameter, in miles (1,391,000 km)
9,000	Average surface temperature, in °F (5,500°C)
6,300	Temperature in the eye of a sunspot, in °F (3,500°C)
1,800,000–3,600,000	Temperature of the corona, in °F (1,000,000–2,000,000°C)
25	Earth days to rotate once (36 days at the poles)
8	Minutes for light to reach Earth

solar activity can mean power and communications disruptions on Earth. (See Chapter Nine for more on auroras.)

You can see very large sunspots with the naked eye (and a filter, of course), but you'll need binoculars to see smaller ones and a small telescope to see other details on the Sun.

Prominences The Sun isn't described as fiery for nothing. The surface is a seething mass of shifting magnetic fields and hot gas. Often, streams of superheated gas—called prominences—will erupt from the Sun's surface and out into space, some for hundreds of thousands of miles.

Unfortunately, you'll need an H-alpha filter to see prominences on the Sun. A cheaper way to see them is to check out a few websites featuring solar imagery. (See the Resources on page 150 for listings.)

Another way to see prominences, along with the ethereal corona, is during a total solar eclipse, when the light of the Sun's bright disk is conveniently blocked by the Moon. You can find out more about solar (and lunar) eclipses in Chapter Eight.

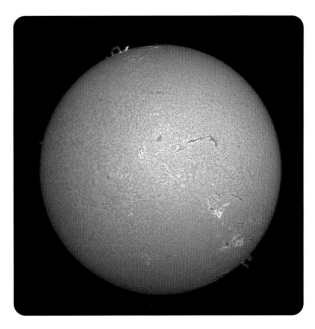

The Sun in Hydrogen-alpha

H-alpha filters are very expensive and not usually part of a beginner's stargazing arsenal. Keen solar observers and photographers, however, prize them for the detail they reveal. In this H-alpha photo, the granular surface of the Sun shows up, as do a couple of large prominences (top and bottom). The white areas are sunspots, and the red tinge circling the solar disc is the chromosphere.

PROJECTS

○ PROJECT 1: Observing Sunspots 1

Using a solar filter, observe the Sun with the unaided eye. What can you see? Can you see any sunspots? Don't be surprised if you don't; they need to be quite large to be visible without binoculars or a telescope. Now try the same thing with filtered binoculars. Check the Sun periodically to see whether sunspots are visible. If they are, note when and where you saw them in your observing log, then track them by observing the Sun on a daily basis, to watch them move. Note when they appear and then disappear and any changes in their size. How many sunspots are there? Do the numbers change?

○ PROJECT 2: Observing Sunspots 2

Using a solar filter, observe the Sun through a telescope. Note the size and shape of the sunspots, their location and number. Track them as they rotate with the Sun. Can you see the umbra? The penumbra? Watch to see whether the spots grow or shrink over time as they move across the solar face.

CHAPTER FIVE
BEYOND THE
SOLAR SYSTEM

You could spend a lot of time observing the solar system. In fact, some amateur astronomers prefer studying the features of the Moon, Sun, and planets. But for others, the thrill of stargazing comes from looking beyond the fringes of the solar system, into the realm of stars, nebulas, and galaxies—what we call the *deep sky*.

Stellar Nursery
Immense clouds of dust and gas drift through space, each one a potential nursery for newborn stars.

First, a Little Background

So, what's out there, anyway?

Stars

The universe is filled with stars—billions of them—in varying colors, sizes, and stages of life. Some are being born, some are dying, some are in their prime. Our Sun is one of these prime-of-life stars, and much of what we know about other stars we've learned from our own. Likewise, what we know about the life cycle of our Sun comes from studying other stars.

Life Cycle of a Star

All stars are born the same way: when a massive cloud of cool, dense gas—called a molecular cloud—collapses inward and forms what is called a *protostar,* a star that has not yet begun to shine. When the hydrogen gas at the center of the protostar comes under enough pressure, it begins the process of nuclear fusion: the star ignites and becomes a main-sequence star. Our Sun is a main-sequence star; that is, it's in the process of turning hydrogen into helium. All stars in this stage of their lives are called *main-sequence* stars.

Not all stars are created equal, however, and it's at this point—when they ignite—that the paths of stars diverge.

Stars like the Sun—with about the same mass (mass is the amount of matter in an object)—burn through their available hydrogen and, after several billion years, begin to die, ending their lives as described in Chapter Four. They swell up into red giants, shrug off their outer shells, and eventually shrink to become white-dwarf stars.

But stars with a mass eight times or greater than that of the Sun—they're called *high-mass* stars; anything with less mass than this is called a *low-mass* star—live entirely different lifestyles. These stars live in the fast lane. Massive, hot, and bright, they burn through their fuel in millions, rather than billions, of years (you might think of them as the James Deans of the universe). They end their lives in spectacular fashion, too. Like the Sun, they begin to expand, but rather than becoming mere red giants, high-mass stars swell up into bloated red *supergiants.* Once they've burned up their last dregs of available fuel, they

Billions and Billions

Countless stars crowd this photo of the constellation of Gemini. The bright blue spot visible at the bottom right of this photo is M35, a lovely open cluster near the western "foot" of Gemini.

explode—violently and brilliantly—in what's called a *supernova.* The material blown off becomes a *nebula* (see page 66), and what remains becomes either a neutron star or a black hole, depending on the star's (pre-explosion) mass.

At the other end of the stellar spectrum are stars with less mass than the Sun. Called *red dwarfs* (never *dwarves*), these stars failed to accumulate enough mass when they formed to shine very brightly. Red dwarfs burn slowly. Some have been around for as long as the universe has been in existence and will probably go on burning for . . . well, forever. Deep space is filled with these types of stars; in fact, they make up the majority of the stellar population. Only a very few red dwarf stars are bright enough to be easily visible in backyard telescopes, however.

Objects with even less mass than a red dwarf fail to become stars at all; they become giant gaseous planets like Jupiter.

Types of Stars

Even though it's often described as such, in one sense, our Sun is not your average star. Why? Because the majority of stars populating our universe have siblings—whereas our Sun is an only child. Most stellar nurseries (those dense clouds of gas) produce a clutch of stars, many of which are connected to each other by a kind of gravitational umbilical cord. We know them as double stars, multiple stars, and star clusters.

Double Stars   Roughly half of the universe's population of stars consists of double stars. Also called *binary* stars, they are two stars that were born together in the stellar cloud nursery. Connected by each other's gravity, the two stars orbit around their common center of mass. Although "twins," the stars are not always the same size. Often, one star is visibly larger and brighter than the other.

Some stars look to us like double stars but, in fact, are not connected to each other in any way. In fact, they're not even close. These are called *optical doubles,* because they only appear from Earth to be close together. With a 6-inch (150-mm) telescope and a good deal of experience, you can observe hundreds of double-star systems (though not all at once, of course).

Death of a Star

A dying star (V838 Monocerotis) sheds its outer shell of dust and gas. As the shell expands and moves out into space, it is illuminated by the bright red supergiant at the center. V838 Monocerotis is about 20,000 light-years from Earth, at the outer edge of the Milky Way Galaxy.

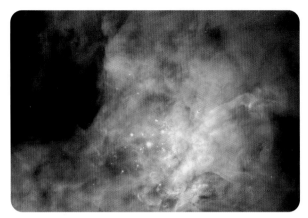

A small cluster of stars nestles in the heart of the Orion Nebula. The four hottest and brightest members are part of a multiple-star system called the Trapezium and are easily seen in a small telescope.

Melotte 111, also known as the Coma Berenices Star Cluster is an open cluster, located in the constellation of Coma Berenices. (See Chapter Six Highlights for how to find it.)

Hundreds of thousands of mostly very old stars comprise M80, a globular cluster about 28,000 light-years from Earth. M80 is one of the densest of the 147 known globular clusters that stud the Milky Way.

Multiple Stars   A multiple-star system can contain three or more stars orbiting a common center of mass, or it can simply be a collection of stars held together by gravity. When you get a large enough collection of stars hanging out with each other, they are considered a cluster.

Star Clusters   Clusters can consist of a few dozen to hundreds of thousands of stars. An *open cluster* is a group of about a dozen to a few hundred young stars. They eventually drift apart (much like teenagers heading off to college). The Pleiades (or Seven Sisters, as it's sometimes called), which is visible to the naked eye, is a young open cluster.

A *globular cluster* is an enormous, densely packed ball of older stars. There may be hundreds of thousands, even millions, of stars in a globular cluster. Like galaxies, stars at their center are even more tightly packed than at the outskirts, giving them a central glow. The Milky Way is studded with about 150 globular clusters. One of the larger ones, the Great Cluster in Hercules, is just visible with the naked eye in a dark sky.

Variable Stars   Variable stars, as their name suggests, are stars whose light level fluctuates. Some stars vary in brightness over time because of changes in their energy output. The brightness of some of these *pulsating variables* changes in less than a day, while others vary over periods of up to several years. The light from other stars changes because they belong to double-star systems oriented edge-on to our line of sight. As the stars orbit each other, one star is temporarily eclipsed when its companion passes in front of it. They're called *eclipsing variables,* and these eclipses can occur once every few hours up to once every couple of decades. Algol in the constellation Perseus is an eclipsing variable, while Delta Cephei, in Cepheus, is a pulsating variable.

THE MAGNITUDE SCALE

Some 2,100 years ago, a Greek astronomer named Hipparchus looked up at the sky and decided to catalog the stars he saw by their brightness. The most brilliant stars he gave a magnitude of 1; the dimmest were designated 6 (yes, it seems backward, but no one has ever changed it), and thus was the magnitude scale born.

The scale has been extended since then, what with the introduction of binoculars and telescopes, which allow us to see many more and fainter objects than Hipparchus could. Negative numbers were added when astronomers discovered that some of Hipparchus's 1st-magnitude stars were actually brighter than others. That's why Sirius, the brightest star in our skies, has a magnitude of –1.4. The brightest object in our sky, at magnitude –27, is the Sun.

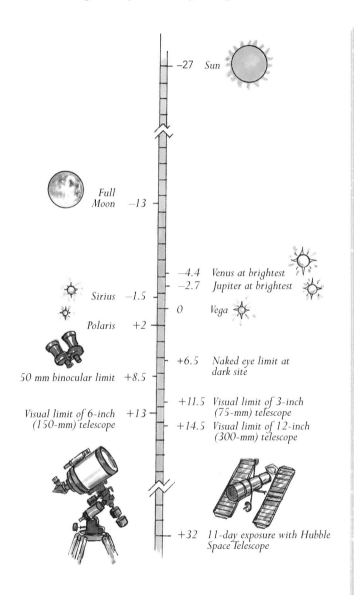

–27	Sun	
–13	Full Moon	
–4.4	Venus at brightest	
–2.7	Jupiter at brightest	
–1.5	Sirius	
0	Vega	
+2	Polaris	
+6.5	Naked eye limit at dark site	
+8.5	50 mm binocular limit	
+11.5	Visual limit of 3-inch (75-mm) telescope	
+13	Visual limit of 6-inch (150-mm) telescope	
+14.5	Visual limit of 12-inch (300-mm) telescope	
+32	11-day exposure with Hubble Space Telescope	

The Top Twenty Brightest Stars

The following are stars that appear brightest, as seen from Earth.

Star	Constellation	Magnitude
Sirius	Canis Major	–1.4
Canopus	Carina	–0.6
Alpha Centauri	Centaurus	0
Arcturus	Boötes	0
Vega	Lyra	0
Capella	Auriga	0.1
Rigel	Orion	0.2
Procyon	Canis Minor	0.4
Betelgeuse	Orion	0.4–1.3
Achernar	Eridanus	0.5
Beta Centauri	Centaurus	0.6
Altair	Aquila	0.8
Aldebaran	Taurus	0.8–1.0
Spica	Virgo	1.0
Antares	Scorpius	1.0
Pollux	Gemini	1.2
Fomalhaut	Piscis Austrinus	1.2
Beta Crucis	Crux	1.2–1.3
Deneb	Cygnus	1.3
Regulus	Leo	1.4

Nebulas

Massive clouds of gas and dust, nebulas are the galaxy's stellar nurseries. Dense, dark, and mostly invisible, they drift through space, until some disturbance causes one to collapse and begin the process of creating stars.

Types of Nebulas

Have you ever heard that saying, "We are all made of star-stuff"? It may sound hokey, but it's true. The universe is the ultimate recycler. And the material that gets recycled most often is the gas and dust of which nebulas are made.

Emission Nebulas   Home to stars still in their infancy, emission nebulas are where stars are now being born. Hydrogen gas in the cloud is heated to fluorescence by radiation from the newly ignited stars, transforming the clouds into the ethereal, jewel-bright objects we see in photographs taken by the Hubble Space Telescope. One of the best examples of an emission nebula is the Orion Nebula.

Reflection Nebulas   Unlike emission nebulas, reflection nebulas emit no light of their own; they simply reflect the light of nearby stars. M78 in Orion is a reflection nebula.

Planetary Nebulas   Contrary to their name, planetary nebulas have nothing to do with planets. They're formed when a dying

Reflection Nebula

The bright cocoon of dust around a cluster of young stars at the center of this photo is N30B, a reflection nebula. Dubbed the "double bubble," the nebula is encased in a larger nebula, called DEM L 106, located in the Large Magellanic Cloud.

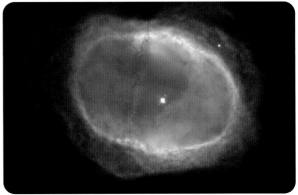

Planetary Nebula

Known as the Southern Ring Nebula, NGC 3132 is a prime example of a planetary nebula—a dying star throwing off a massive shell of gas. At 2,000 light-years distant, it's one of the nearest known planetary nebulas, but it is only visible in southern skies.

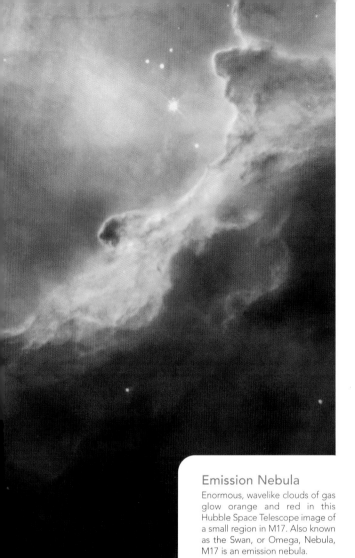

star sheds its outer layers into space. The cloud of ejected gas and dust from the expired star drifts off to join other nebulous clouds and becomes the raw material for the formation of new stars. The Ring Nebula is an example of a planetary nebula.

Supernova Remnants   As the name suggests, supernova remnants are just that: the shredded remains of exploded stars. Like planetary nebulas, this material drifts through space, eventually connecting with other clouds of gas. The Crab Nebula is a beautiful example of a supernova remnant from a star that exploded in AD 1054.

Dark Nebulas   Not all nebulas are like the glorious, rose- and blue-colored celestial objects, whose images you see in coffee-table books. In fact, most are dark, dense clouds that are scattered throughout the galaxy. You can see these dark nebulas when you look up at the summer Milky Way; they're the lanes of dark dust and gas that obscure the light of the stars behind them. A fine example of a dark nebula in the winter sky is the Horsehead Nebula.

Emission Nebula
Enormous, wavelike clouds of gas glow orange and red in this Hubble Space Telescope image of a small region in M17. Also known as the Swan, or Omega, Nebula, M17 is an emission nebula.

Supernova Remnants
These delicate filaments of dust are actually sheets of debris from a stellar explosion in the Large Magellanic Cloud. Named DEM L 190, the remnant is from a massive star that died in a supernova blast whose light reached us thousands of years ago.

Dark Nebula
Rising like the Creature from the Black Lagoon, the Cone Nebula is actually no more than a pillar of cold, dense gas and dust—a dark nebula.

Galaxies

Unlike *Star Trek* captains Kirk, Picard, or Janeway, we don't have a handy version of the starship *Enterprise* to whisk us far enough into space to look back on our own galaxy. The best we can do, from our position deep inside one of its spiral arms, is to look at what's around us and then look beyond, to other galaxies, to see what we can learn from them.

Until the 1920s, most astronomers believed the Milky Way was the only galaxy adrift in the vast ocean of space. Boy, were they wrong! We now know that our swirling city of stars is only one of more than thirty galaxies that make up what's called the Local Group. And that the Local Group is but a small part of an even larger cluster of galaxies called the Virgo Supercluster—which is part of an immense collection of superclusters. In fact, astronomers estimate the number of galaxies in our universe to be in the billions!

Although the numbers may seem mind-boggling, one thing is certain: there's no shortage of subjects to study in our quest to learn more about ourselves.

Types of Galaxies

Spiral Spiral galaxies are like our own—a *nucleus* of tightly packed stars in the center, surrounded by a spherical *bulge* of stars and a rotating disk of spiral arms, rather like an octopus giving itself a hug. Spiral galaxies contain a mix of old and new stars; the older ones are largely concentrated in the glowing bulge and nucleus, while both young and old stars are scattered throughout the spiral arms. It's in the arms, too, that you find many nebulas and the dark lanes of dust.

Edge-On Galaxy

Resembling the hat for which it was named, the Sombrero Galaxy is one of the universe's more photogenic galaxies. A spiral galaxy, the Sombrero's arms are seen here edge-on, giving us an excellent view of its glowing central bulge and dark dust lanes.

Galaxies Galore

It may be hard to imagine, but this image, taken by the Hubble Space Telescope Advanced Camera for Surveys shows a patch of sky $^1/_{10}$ the diameter of the full Moon that, when viewed with a small, backyard telescope, appears to be nothing but empty space. The image, a composite of 800 exposures taken over the course of 400 orbits around the Earth, represents a "core sample" of the universe; that is, a narrow, deep view of space (like looking through a straw), rather than the wide, shallow views we're used to seeing. Some *10,000* galaxies of all shapes and sizes fill this image.

CLASSES OF STARS

You may have heard the Sun described as a G-type star. No, we're not talking about movie classifications. In astronomy, a star's class is defined by its color and temperature. Below is a table of spectral classes of stars. (Temperatures are approximate.)

Class	Color	Temperature	Example
O	Blue	45,000°F and greater (25,000°C)	Lambda Orionis
B	Blue-White	19,000°F–45,000°F (10,500–25,000°C)	Rigel, Spica
A	White	13,000°F–19,000°F (7,200–10,500°C)	Sirius, Vega
F	Yellow-White	10,300°F–13,000°F (5,700°C–7,200°C)	Canopus, Procyon
G	Yellow	8,500°F–10,300°F (4,700°C–5,700°C)	Sun, Capella
K	Orange	5,800°F–8,500 (3,200°C–4,700°C)	Arcturus, Aldebaran
M	Red	less than 5,800°F (3,200°C)	Betelgeuse, Antares

CATALOGING THE DEEP SKY

Have you ever wondered what those M and NGC designations meant?

Back in the eighteenth century, from 1758 to 1782, a French astronomer named Charles Messier compiled a list of fuzzy celestial objects that could be mistaken for comets. (Messier was a comet hunter.) This became the Messier Catalog, in which all 110 objects are designated with an M and a number (some also have a "common" name). Deep-sky object number 31, for example, is M31—the Andromeda Galaxy—and M27 is the Dumbbell Nebula. Of course, there are more than 110 objects in the sky, so in 1887, the New General Catalogue, or NGC, was compiled, listing some 13,000 objects, all with, as you might guess, an NGC prefix. The Rosette Nebula, for example, is NGC 2237. Are the Messier objects in the NGC Catalogue too? Yes. Which is why the Orion Nebula is M42, but it's also NGC 1976. You might also come across an object labeled with an IC —these are listed in the Index Catalogue, one of two supplements to the New General Catalogue.

Spiral Galaxy

The Hubble Space Telescope captured this image of a spiral galaxy similar to our own Milky Way. NGC 4414, as it's named, is about 60 million light-years from Earth.

Although most spiral galaxies have spherical centers, about 30 percent have bar-shaped centers. These are called barred spirals. The size and shape of spiral galaxies can vary, as well. Some have a prominent central bulge and little disk; others are all disk and very little bulge. And some, like the Milky Way and our nearest neighbor, the Andromeda Galaxy, fall somewhere in between.

Elliptical   Unlike spirals, elliptical galaxies have no arms. They look more like a spiral galaxy's central bulge—a sphere of mostly older stars. Some are more flattened—or ellipsoid—in shape than others. Elliptical galaxies do not rotate; in fact, the stars within them orbit the central bulge in different directions. Astronomers now think that ellipticals are formed from the collision and eventual merger of two spiral galaxies.

Irregular   Irregular galaxies, as you might guess, belong to neither of the aforementioned categories. These galaxies lack a discernible nucleus and any sort of organized structure. You might think of them as extremely massive star clusters. While spiral galaxies consist of a mix of old and young stars, and ellipticals are largely made up of older stars, irregular galaxies are where the younger crowd hang out—there's lots of star formation happening here. The Large and Small Clouds of Magellan are examples of irregular galaxies.

Irregular Galaxies

The two fuzzy shapes in this image are actually the Large and Small Clouds of Magellan. Our next-door neighbors in space, the Clouds are good examples of irregular galaxies. Both are visible to the naked eye from southern latitudes.

PROJECTS

○ PROJECT 1: Find the Brightest Stars

Check out the list of Top Twenty Brightest Stars on page 65. See how many stars you can find, and check them off as you go. Some stars can only be seen from southern latitudes, so you may have to do some traveling to complete the project.

○ PROJECT 2: Star Colors

Using the same list, note the colors of the stars. If you can't see a star's color with the naked eye, try observing it through binoculars or a small telescope; the color may become apparent.

○ PROJECT 3: Find Double Stars

Flip ahead to Chapter Six and find out how to locate the double stars listed in the Highlights; you may want to start with Albireo, one of the easier double stars to find. Using binoculars, see how many double stars you can observe. Once you've found those listed in Chapter Six, use the sky maps to see where other double stars are located (there's a symbol on the legend to help you) and see how many more you can discover.

○ PROJECT 4: Observe Algol and Monitor its Brightness

Flip ahead to Chapter Six and find the Highlights for November/December, then use the sky map to find Algol, an eclipsing binary star whose brightness fades for a few hours every 2.87 days, as one star passes in front of the other. Its changes are clearly visible to the naked eye: at mid-eclipse it dims to magnitude 3.4 from its usual magnitude of 2.1 (remember, the magnitude scale is the reverse of what you'd expect—the larger the number, the dimmer the object). Compare Algol's brightness to the 2.1-magnitude star immediately to its west—that last bright star in the curve of Andromeda. If Algol looks fainter, then it's probably in eclipse. (For more on Algol and its predicted minimums, check out *www.SkyandTelescope.com.*) Observing Algol can be done most of the year, though the star is very low in the north during summer evenings.

○ PROJECT 5: Observe Delta Cephei and Monitor its Brightness

Flip ahead to Chapter Six and find the Highlights for November/December, then use the sky map to find Delta Cephei, a pulsating variable star, whose brightness fluctuates from magnitude 3.5 to 4.3 over a short period of 5 ⅓ days. The star rises quickly to maximum brilliancy, then slowly fades to minimum. Find the two stars close to Delta: the brighter one is magnitude 3.4, the fainter is 4.2. You can see all three of these stars together in binoculars, and, by using the other two stars as a reference, you can follow Delta's changing brightness over time. Over several consecutive evenings, note when Delta looks as bright as one star, as faint as the other, or somewhere in between. Can you estimate Delta's magnitude? Note your observations in your observing log, along with the date and time you made the observation. Although Delta Cephei is listed in the November/December Highlights, you can observe it most of the year; it's a little more difficult to find during spring, though, when it's very low in the north.

CHAPTER SIX
BACKYARD STARGAZING

ow that you know what's out there, you'll want to know how to find—and where and when to look for—these fascinating celestial objects. In this chapter, you'll learn how to read and use the six sky maps on the following pages, as well as how to use familiar constellations and asterisms to locate less-familiar constellations, stars, and deep-sky objects. And with each star map, we'll highlight some easy-to-find celestial sights that you can see with the naked eye, binoculars, or a small telescope.

Where do you begin? With the constellations.

The Summer Triangle peeks through the trees in this photo of a summer night sky.

THE CONSTELLATIONS

First, a Little Background

Look up at the night sky—especially a dark one—and the first thing you may notice (once you've become dark-adapted) is just how many stars you can see. Even more were visible in the days before light pollution, when the ancients were studying the skies. In an attempt to make some sense of the 3,000 or so stars they could see up there, stargazers of old arranged them into patterns called constellations.

They weren't the same constellations for everyone, however. Each culture—Greek, Roman, Egyptian, and Chinese—had its own patterns of stars and names for them. The names by which we know the constellations today are based on Latin translations of the names given to them by the Greeks, who gave them the names of mythological figures. (They're also known by more common translations: Boötes, for example, is called the Herdsman. See the Constellations table on page 80.)

Of course, once telescopes came along, even more stars became visible, so modern-day astronomers decided to organize the sky into universally recognized boundaries. Starting with the already-established constellations, they divided the sky into eighty-eight sections, each containing the familiar patterns we see, plus a whole lot of stars we can't see, with the naked eye. (Think of each constellation as a state or province; within its boundaries are major cities—the stars we see—and many more smaller towns and villages—the stars we can't see). Every star in the sky, visible or not, is part of a constellation. Three-quarters of them can be seen from the Northern Hemisphere; the others are only visible in southern skies. So, if you want to check Toucana off on your constellations life-list, you'll need to head south of the equator.

If you've scanned the list of constellations and can't find the Big Dipper on it, that's because the Big Dipper isn't a constellation; it's an *asterism,* a recognizable pattern of stars that has no "official" status. The Summer Triangle, the Great Square of Pegasus, the Northern Cross: all of these are asterisms. The Big Dipper (known as the Plough in Britain) is actually part of the constellation of Ursa Major, the Great Bear.

Where to Look: Navigating the Night Sky

"All right," you're thinking, "so the sky has been divided into sections, but the real sky doesn't come with lines and road signs. How on Earth do I find anything up there?"

STAR NAMES

Aldebaran, Bellatrix, Betelgeuse, Zubenelgenubi: some stars have pretty strange names. How did they get them?

Not surprisingly, it was the Babylonians (the same folks who first identified the zodiac and named the constellations) who first gave names to the stars. In the centuries that followed, Arab and Greek astronomers threw their hats into the star-naming ring, as well. As a result, the names by which we now know the major stars are mostly Greek and Arabic, with some Latin and Persian thrown in.

Not all stars have such colorful names (or colorful meanings: Betelgeuse, for example, means "armpit of the central one"). Only the brightest (about seventy-five to one hundred) bear "proper" names.

So, what happens when we want to refer to "the fourth-brightest star in the constellation of Cepheus"? We call it Delta Cephei. We call it that because of a system developed back in 1603 by a German astronomer named Johannes Bayer, who allocated Greek letters to the main stars in each constellation in order of brightness, alpha being the brightest, beta the next brightest, and so on. So, Alpha Centauri? Yes—it's the brightest star in the constellation of Centaurus.

These Greek designations don't appear on the Sky Maps starting on page 84 in this book, but most detailed maps do show the Greek symbol next to the brighter stars in each constellation. Here's a list for future reference.

The Greek Alphabet

α	alpha	ι	iota	ρ	rho
β	beta	κ	kappa	σ	sigma
γ	gamma	λ	lambda	τ	tau
δ	delta	μ	mu	υ	upsilon
ε	epsilon	ν	nu	φ	phi
ζ	zeta	ξ	xi	χ	chi
η	eta	o	omicron	ψ	psi
θ	theta	π	pi	ω	omega

Answer? Get to know the constellations. While you could spend a lot of time learning about right ascension and declination to figure out where the Ring Nebula is (and one day you might), you may find it easier to just check out a sky map and see that it's located in Lyra. And when you know where to find

Lyra in the sky, you'll know where to look for the Ring Nebula. Simple, right?

Once you're familiar with the constellations, you can employ a handy little trick called *star hopping*: using an easy-to-spot, naked-eye starting point—such as a bright star in a constellation—and then a series of short visual "hops" to find a fainter object. (See the highlights in the Sky Maps section [on page 82] for examples.)

Signpost Constellations

Two of the first star patterns to get to know—and you're probably already familiar with them—are the Big Dipper and Orion. Why these two? Because they're what we call signposts. Using just these two star groupings, you can find your way to every major constellation visible in the northern sky (see illustrations). Although Orion is not visible in the evening sky from late April to early November, the Big Dipper can be seen throughout the year by anyone living north of 40 degrees latitude.

Using the seven stars in the Big Dipper, you can find the

Big Dipper Signpost

The Big Dipper is visible year-round for anyone living north of 40 degrees latitude. Use the Dipper to find your way to several bright stars and constellations.

Orion Signpost

Use Orion from December to April to find your way around the winter sky.

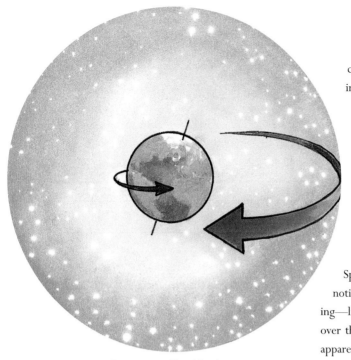

Apparent Sky Motion

constellation of Cassiopeia and the bright stars Arcturus, in Boötes; Spica, in Virgo; Regulus, in Leo; Deneb, in Cygnus; Vega, in Lyra; and Castor and Pollux, in Gemini, as well as Polaris, the North Star, in the Little Dipper (also an asterism). Orion's pointer stars will show you the way to the Pleiades star cluster, in Taurus; and the bright stars Sirius, in Canis Major; Castor and Pollux, in Gemini; Aldebaran, in Taurus; Procyon, in Canis Minor; and Capella, in Auriga.

When to Look: Motions of the Stars

Spend an evening under the stars, and you'll probably notice that they don't stand still. They wheel overhead, rising—like the Sun—in the east and dropping, many hours later, over the horizon in the west. Early astronomers noticed this apparent motion, too—which is why they firmly believed that a sphere of stars revolved around the Earth.

SEASONAL STARS
Why Constellations Change Seasonally

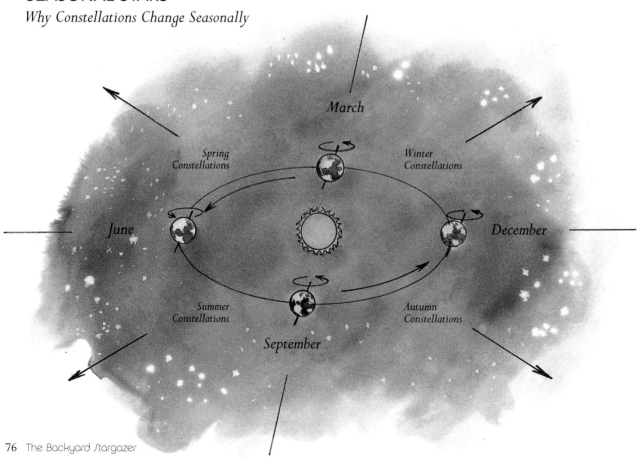

Star Trails

It may look like the photographer jiggled the camera in this photo, but, in fact, it's the stars—those bright streaks of light—that have moved. (See Apparent Sky Motion for more on this.) Note the bright spot in the center of the circles—this is Polaris, which hardly moves at all. Also known as the North or Pole Star, Polaris is located, as you might guess, almost directly above the Earth's north pole. Stars that circle Polaris and never drop below the horizon are called circumpolar stars.

We've since learned, of course, that the opposite is true: the stars are fixed in space (well, they do move, but so slowly, it takes thousands of years to notice a change), and it's the Earth that rotates. Each day, as the Earth rotates from west to east, the stars appear to move from east to west. (See Apparent Sky Motion illustration.) This daily "movement" of the stars is called *apparent sky motion.*

Why should you care about apparent sky motion? Because where the stars are in their daily journey will determine when you can see them. If you had your heart set on observing Orion, for example, you'll want to be sure it's above the horizon during the evening hours.

Constellations change during the course of the year, as well. Looking for Orion in mid-July will prove disappointing, as Orion is only visible during the evenings from December to late April. Why?

Because of something called *annual motion.* As the Earth revolves around the Sun, it moves through different parts of the sky, so a person looking out from our planet will see different constellations at various times of the year. The part of the sky that Orion is in, for example, is only visible to us when the night side of the Earth is facing that part of the sky—in winter. (See Seasonal Stars illustration.)

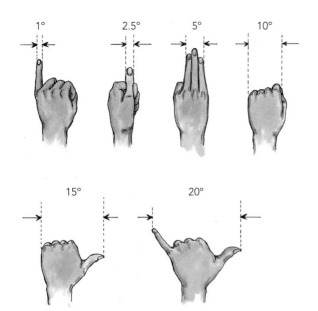

THE CELESTIAL SPHERE

If someone asked you where Abu Dhabi was and you didn't know, you'd do one of two things: guess (if you were on a game show), or look it up on a map. But, what if you want to find out where a star is located? Yes, you look for it on a map of the sky.

How does one map the sky? By plotting the positions of celestial objects on what astronomers call the celestial sphere, an imaginary globe surrounding the Earth. "Drawn" on this sphere is a celestial grid of imaginary lines—extensions of those on Earth: an equator, called (naturally) the *celestial equator,* and lines of *right ascension* (longitude) and *declination* (latitude). Lying directly above the north and south poles are the north and south *celestial poles.* Circling the celestial sphere is the *ecliptic.*

SKY MEASURES

Measuring distances between objects using degrees is another way of finding your way around the sky. It was the Babylonians who devised this system, dividing the celestial sphere into 360 degrees. (Think of the sky above you as a snow globe, with the horizon as its base. The measurement around the base, or circumference, is 360 degrees. The measurement from the base over the dome and back down to the base is 180 degrees.)

So, how do you measure degrees in the sky? You use your hands and fingers. Here's how. (See illustration.)

Hold your hand up at arm's length. Now, hold up just your little finger. The width of the end of your little finger is 1 degree. Three fingers held up (in a Boy Scout salute) spans 5 degrees, and your fist spans 10 degrees. Sticking your thumb out expands the width to 15 degrees, and your hand with fingers spread measures about 20 to 25 degrees, from fingertip to fingertip (depending on how far you can spread your fingers).

But wait, you're thinking, hands come in different sizes. Yes, but so do arm lengths, and people with small hands generally have shorter arms.

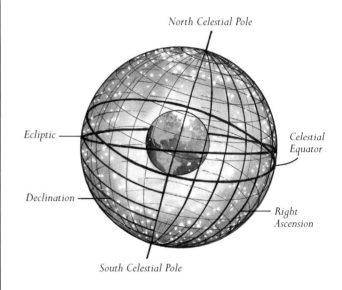

THE ZODIAC

"Aha!" you're thinking. "I already know what the zodiac is. I'm a Leo. Next topic!"

Okay, so you probably do know what the zodiac is, as it relates to astrology. But do you know what the zodiac is in astronomy? Remember, astrology and astronomy parted ways a good long time ago, and you want to be sure never to mix the two up.

In astronomy, the zodiac describes the constellations that lie along the ecliptic. While there are twelve constellations in the astrological zodiac, thirteen constellations cross the ecliptic. The one you've likely never heard of is Ophiuchus, the Serpent Bearer. Zodiacal constellations are easy to find on the star maps: you just look for them along the ecliptic, which is marked on each map.

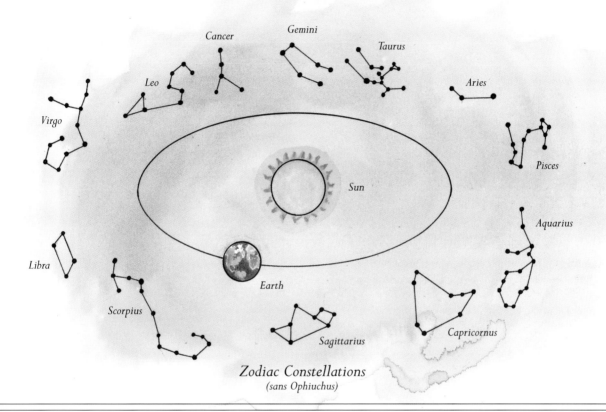

Zodiac Constellations
(sans Ophiuchus)

PROJECT

○ PROJECT 1: Practice Sky Measures

Make a copy of the sky measures and put them into practice. Use them to measure the width of the Moon, distances between bright stars, and the distance between an object and the horizon. Note them in your observing log, if you like. Sky measures will come in handy later on, when you begin using them to find objects in the night sky.

THE CONSTELLATIONS

The following is a list of all eighty-eight constellations. Some are visible only from the Northern Hemisphere, some only from the Southern Hemisphere, and some can be seen from both hemispheres, depending on the time of year. Use it as a kind of life list, checking off each one as you come to recognize and know it over your observing career.

Name	Abbreviation	Pronunciation	Meaning
Andromeda	And	an-DROM-e-da	Daughter of Cassiopeia
Antlia	Ant	ANT-lee-uh	Air Pump
Apus	Aps	A-pus	Bird of Paradise
Aquarius	Aqr	uh-KWER-e-us	Water bearer
Aquila	Aql	uh-KWIL-uh	Eagle
Ara	Ara	A-ruh	Altar
Aries	Ari	AIR-eez	Ram
Auriga	Aur	or-EE-guh	Charioteer
Boötes	Boo	bo-OH-teez	Herdsman
Caelum	Cae	SEE-lum	Chisel
Camelopardalis	Cam	ka-MEL-o-PAR-da-lis	Giraffe
Cancer	Cnc	KAN-ser	Crab
Canes Venatici	Cvn	KA-nez ve-NAT-icee	Hunting Dogs
Canis Major	CMa	KA-nis MA-jer	Big Dog
Canis Minor	CMi	KA-nis MI-ner	Little Dog
Capricornus	Cap	KAP-ri-KORN-us	Goat
Carina	Car	kuh-REE-nuh	Keel
Cassiopeia	Cas	CAS-ee-o-PEE-yuh	Queen
Centaurus	Cen	sen-TOR-us	Centaur
Cepheus	Cep	SEE-fee-yus	King
Cetus	Cet	SEE-tus	Whale
Chamaeleon	Cha	kuh-MEE-lee-yun	Chameleon
Circinus	Cir	SER-sin-us	Compasses
Columba	Col	koh-LUM-buh	Dove
Coma Berenices	Com	KOH-muh ber-e-NEE-seez	Berenice's Hair
Corona Australis	CrA	ko-ROH-nuh aus-TRA-lis	Southern Crown
Corona Borealis	CrB	ko-RO-nuh bor-ee-AL-is	Northern Crown
Corvus	Crv	KOR-vus	Crow
Crater	Crt	KRAY-ter	Cup
Crux	Cru	KRUKS	Cross
Cygnus	Cyg	SIG-nus	Swan
Delphinus	Del	del-FIN-us	Dolphin
Dorado	Dor	Do-ROD-oh	Swordfish
Draco	Dra	DRAY-ko	Dragon
Equuleus	Equ	ee-KWOO-lee-us	Little Horse
Eridanus	Eri	ee-RID-a-nus	River
Fornax	For	FOR-naks	Furnace
Gemini	Gem	JEM-i-ni	Twins
Grus	Gru	grus	Crane (bird)
Hercules	Her	HER-cue-leez	The Strongman
Horologium	Hor	hor-oh-LO-jee-um	Clock
Hydra	Hya	HI-dra	Water Snake (Female)

Name	Abbreviation	Pronunciation	Meaning
Hydrus	Hyi	HI-drus	Water Snake (Male)
Indus	Ind	IN-dus	Indian
Lacerta	Lac	luh-SER-tuh	Lizard
Leo	Leo	LEE-oh	Lion
Leo Minor	LMi	LEE-oh MI-ner	Little Lion
Lepus	Lep	LEE-pus	Hare
Libra	Lib	LEE-bruh	Balance
Lupus	Lup	LOO-pus	Wolf
Lynx	Lyn	links	Lynx
Lyra	Lyr	LI-ruh	Lyre
Mensa	Men	MEN-suh	Table
Microscopium	Mic	MI-kro-SCOPE-ee-um	Microscope
Monoceros	Mon	mon-OSS-er-us	Unicorn
Musca	Mus	MUS-kuh	Fly
Norma	Nor	NOR-muh	Square
Octans	Oct	OCK-tanz	Octant
Ophiuchus	Oph	OH-fee-U-kus	Serpent bearer
Orion	Ori	o-RI-un	Hunter
Pavo	Pav	PAY-voh	Peacock
Pegasus	Peg	PEG-uh-sus	Winged Horse
Perseus	Per	PER-see-us	Rescuer of Andromeda
Phoenix	Phe	FEE-nix	Phoenix
Pictor	Pic	PIC-ter	Painter
Pisces	Psc	PI-seez	Fishes
Pisces Austrinus	PsA	PI-seez os-TRI-nus	Southern Fish
Puppis	Pup	PUP-is	Stern
Pyxis	Pyx	PIK-sis	Compass
Reticulum	Ret	re-TIK-u-lum	Reticle
Sagitta	Sge	suh-JIT-uh	Arrow
Sagittarius	Sgr	sa-ji-TARE-ee-us	Archer
Scorpius	Sco	SKOR-pe-us	Scorpion
Sculptor	Scl	SKULP-ter	Sculptor
Scutum	Sct	SKEW-tum	Shield
Serpens	Ser	SER-pens	Serpent
Sextans	Sex	SEKS-tans	Sextant
Taurus	Tau	TOR-us	Bull
Telescopium	Tel	tele-SCOPE-ee-um	Telescope
Triangulum	Tri	tri-ANG-gu-lum	Triangle
Triangulum Australe	TrA	tri-ANG-gu-lum aus-TRA-lee	Southern Triangle
Toucana	Tuc	too-KAN-uh	Toucan
Ursa Major	UMa	ER-sa MA jer	Great Bear
Ursa Minor	UMi	ER-sa MI-ner	Little Bear
Vela	Vel	VEE-luh	Sails
Virgo	Vir	VER-go	Maiden
Volans	Vol	VO-lanz	Flying Fish
Vulpecula	Vul	vul-PEK-u-luh	Fox

THE SKY MAPS

On the following pages, you'll find six bimonthly star maps that will help you find and learn the constellations throughout the year. They will become your best friends as you get to know the sky. The maps also show you where to look for some of the brighter deep-sky objects—galaxies, star clusters, and nebulas—plus other sights, such as double stars and variable stars. What you won't find on the star maps are positions of the Moon and planets, since they change from month to month and year to year. You'll want to check an astronomy website or a magazine with monthly star maps for the current positions of these objects. Astronomy software that will do the same thing is also available (see Resources).

On the page opposite each sky map, you'll find a list of celestial highlights, including deep-sky objects, to look for during each bimonthly period. They range from easy-to-find to more difficult. Some objects can be seen with the naked eye; to see others, you may need binoculars or a small telescope. Start with the naked-eye sights, like constellations and bright stars, then add binocular sights. Once you've gotten to know your way around the constellations, think about investing in a telescope, so you can investigate the deep sky—by then, you'll have learned where to point it.

NOTE: Most of the deep-sky objects described on the following pages as visible to the naked eye can be seen only in a dark sky, away from city lights.

How to Use the Maps

They may look a little intimidating, but once you've figured them out, star maps are easy to use. Here's how.

1. Pick out the map for the current month. If it's May, turn to the May/June map. Note that each map lists a range of observing times. These mean that, within an hour or so of those times, what you see on the map will match what you see in the sky. Also noted in the bar just below each map is a small legend, showing star magnitudes and icons for the deep-sky objects.

2. Now take a look at the directions written around the perimeter of the map: Facing South, Facing West, and so on. When you use the map, hold it so that the direction you're facing appears at the bottom of the map. For example, if you are facing west, hold the map so that Facing West is at the bottom. The stars shown from the bottom edge of the map—the horizon—up to the center, the overhead point called the zenith (it's labeled), are the stars you will see in the sky above and in front of you. Stars on the map above the zenith are actually behind you, in the eastern sky, so ignore those for now. (It helps to think of the map as a dome, rather than a flat piece of paper.)

3. Okay, now try it outside. If you're wondering how to find west, remember that west is where the Sun sets. So, if west is in front of you, east will be behind you; south is to your left, and north is to your right. (You'll get the hang of it.)

Of course, the constellations in the sky will be much larger than on the map—and they won't have those helpful connecting lines, but if you keep at it, you'll begin to see the constellations with ease.

Things to remember:

• Use a red-light flashlight for reading the star maps while observing

• Get dark adapted; the longer you stay outside, away from bright lights, the more you will see

• When you're ready, think about starting an observing log (see Chapter One); it will be interesting to look back on these beginning forays into stargazing once you become an experienced observer

• Once you graduate to a telescope, consider buying a good star atlas, which will give you more detailed maps of the sky and will help you find many of the fainter deep-sky sights

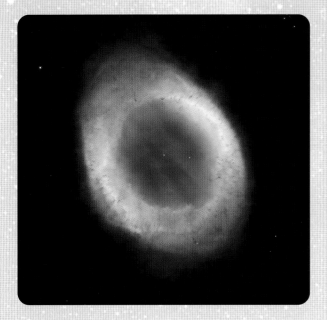

The Ring Nebula, as captured by the Hubble Space Telescope, left, and as you'd see it through a small telescope, right.

THE EYE VS. THE CAMERA

Many beginner stargazers are disappointed the first time they spot a deep-sky object through binoculars or a telescope. "Where," they complain, "are the colors? Why does the nebula/star cluster/galaxy look so small? Why doesn't it look like it does in the pictures?"

It's a case of great expectations. The pictures in the magazines and coffee-table books and calendars can be breathtaking, and, naturally, that's what we expect to see. So, it can be disheartening to put your eye up to the scope and see only a faint blur of light against a dark background. Unfortunately, our eyes are not sensitive enough to the faint light emitted by these objects to pick up color. Film, on the other hand, is—especially if the photographer takes a long exposure; the shutter stays open for a few minutes or more, all the while gathering light. (Planets are the exception to the no-color rule.)

What the pictures don't give you is that sense of awe that you get when you realize that you are looking at an object that is thousands or even millions of light-years away. Anybody can look at a picture—you're looking at the real thing.

A Note about Latitudes

The sky maps are drawn for observers at mid-northern latitudes, that is, from about 35°N to 45°N in North America, Europe, and Asia. If you live south of 35°N, you will see more stars and constellations in the southern sky, and they will appear higher than on the map. The stars and constellations in the north will appear lower in the sky (or may not be visible at all.) If you live north of 45°N, you will see more stars and constellations in the northern sky, and they will appear higher than on the map. The stars and constellations in the south will appear lower in the sky (or may not be visible at all). Stars and constellations in the east and west remain the same.

Face the northern horizon and hold the map so that Facing North is at the bottom. Now look up and find the **Big Dipper**, the asterism in **Ursa Major**, the Great Bear. It'll be high in the sky, very near the zenith. Note the three bright stars that make up the Dipper's handle; from the bowl outward they are Alioth, Mizar, and Alkaid. Focus your attention on **Mizar**, the middle star, at the bend in the handle. If your eyes are particularly sharp, you'll see that Mizar is a double star—a second star, **Alcor**, is nestled close beside it. Mizar and Alcor are an optical double, visually close but not gravitationally connected. Binoculars will show the separation clearly, while a small telescope will reveal that Mizar is itself a binary star system.

While facing the Big Dipper, find the pair of stars at the end of the bowl: Dubhe and, just above it, Merak. These are known as the "pointer stars." Draw a line down from those two stars until you come to a medium-bright star. This is **Polaris**, the North Star (also known as the Pole Star). Note that it's not a particularly bright star, as it's often mistakenly believed to be. Observe it during the course of an evening, and you'll see that all the other stars move around it, while Polaris remains fixed in place. Polaris is the last in a series of three stars that makes up the handle of the **Little Dipper**, an asterism that comprises most of **Ursa Minor**, the Little Bear.

Use the Big Dipper (top, left) to find Polaris, the North Star, in the handle of the Little Dipper (bottom, right).

As spring arrives in the northern hemisphere, so does the constellation of **Leo**, the Lion. To find him, look south, hold the map so that Facing South is at the bottom, and look way up past the zenith to the Big Dipper. Let your gaze drop straight down from the bowl until you encounter six stars that appear to be a backward question mark. This is the **Sickle**, an asterism in Leo, which forms the front quarters of the Lion. The bright star at the handle of the Sickle (or the front paw of the Lion) is **Regulus**, Leo's brightest star. Regulus lies almost right on the ecliptic, so the Moon and planets frequently pass near this star.

Now hold the map so that Facing West is at the bottom, and turn so you're looking west. About two-thirds of the way up from the horizon is a pair of bright stars. These are **Castor** (on the right) and **Pollux**, in the constellation of **Gemini**, the Twins. Characters from Greek mythology, Castor and Pollux were the brothers of Helen of Troy. These Twins are not identical, however; binoculars reveal that they differ in color—Pollux has an orange hue, while Castor is white. A medium-sized scope (using high power) aimed at Castor shows another difference. Castor is a binary star. In fact, Castor is a six-star system, but only this bright pair is easy to see. We're not done with Gemini, though. Scan down to the foot of the right Twin; here, you'll find **M35**, a pretty open cluster visible as a grainy patch through binoculars and fully resolved in a telescope.

Turn the map slightly so that Facing SW is at the bottom. Halfway between Gemini and Leo, along the ecliptic, is **Cancer**, the Crab, a rather faint and unimpressive zodiacal constellation. Hidden within it, however, is a jewel: **M44**, the **Beehive Cluster**, an open cluster, which, as its name suggests, looks much like a swarm of bees. Under dark skies, stargazers with good eyesight should be able to make it out without optical aid. Binoculars, however, show it off to best advantage.

Star magnitudes
−1 0 1 2 3 4

Variable star · Double star · Open cluster · Globular cluster · Galaxy · Planetary nebula · Diffuse nebula

Facing South

Other March/April sights: The **Lyrid** meteor shower peaks on April 22. The radiant is located in the tiny constellation of Lyra, which rises after midnight.

When to use this map

Early March: 11 PM
Late March: 10 PM
Early April: 10 PM*
Late April: Dusk

The chart is also useful in early December at 5 AM, early January at 3 AM, and early February at 1 AM.

Daylight saving time

start your early summer observing session by locating the Big Dipper. Face the western horizon and hold the map so that Facing West is at the bottom. You'll find the Big Dipper about two-thirds of the way up from the horizon to the zenith (and a little to your right). Notice that the handle of the Big Dipper has a slight curve to it. Follow that arc to the left; keep going until you come to a bright star. This is **Arcturus**, a 0-magnitude star in the constellation of **Boötes**, the Herdsman. Note its orange color. If you continue the arc past Arcturus, you'll come to another bright star, blue-white **Spica**, in the constellation of **Virgo**, the Maiden. (A clever way to find these two stars is to remember to "arc to Arcturus" and "speed on to Spica.") Spica is very close to the ecliptic, so you'll sometimes see the Moon and planets pass near this bright star.

Change directions: turn to face south and hold the map so Facing South is at the bottom. Gaze high to find Arcturus again, then look to its upper left to the next bright star in Boötes. This is **Epsilon Boötis**, a double star. You'll need a small telescope to split it into its two component stars. Further to the upper left of Arcturus is the constellation **Corona Borealis**, the Northern Crown, recognizable as a pretty little semi circlet of stars.

Now use binoculars to scan to the right of Arcturus into the constellation of **Coma Berenices** (Berenice's Hair). You should see a small collection of stars just about where the "es" in Berenices is written on the star map. This is the **Coma Berenices Star Cluster**, an open cluster also known as **Melotte 111**. If you have very good eyesight—and a very dark sky—you might be able to just make out the cluster with the naked eye. It's not a compact cluster: its stars are scattered over an area that's about nine times the diameter of the full Moon, so it's best seen in binoculars, which will give you a wider field of view than a telescope.

Immediately below Corona Borealis is the constellation of **Serpens Caput**, which means "head of the serpent." Look for the brightest star in the serpent's neck. Just below and to the right of that star is **M5**, a globular star cluster. It's visible in binoculars but is particularly striking in a small telescope.

Very close to the southeastern horizon, you'll see a bright

Bright and easy to see in binoculars is M13, a globular cluster in Hercules.

star rising. This is **Antares**, near the head of **Scorpius**, the Scorpion. Antares is a 1st-magnitude star, notable for its reddish orange color. In fact, its name means "rival of Mars." Just to the right of Antares, visible in binoculars or a small telescope, is a globular cluster, **M4**.

Finally, face east and rotate the map so that Facing East is at the bottom. See three bright stars above the horizon? They form the **Summer Triangle**, an asterism better seen during the summer. The uppermost (and brightest) star is **Vega**. Draw a line from Vega toward Arcturus, but stop about a third of the way along in the constellation of **Hercules**, the Strongman. Find the irregular square of stars that forms the body of Hercules; it's sometimes known as the Keystone of Hercules. Use binoculars to search between the two uppermost stars of this keystone for a faint, round, fuzzy patch of light. This is the lovely globular cluster **M13**. A medium-sized scope will resolve this glow into myriad pinpoints of light.

To the left of the Keystone, near a foot of Hercules, is another globular cluster: **M92**, which is often overlooked because it's so close to its better-known neighbor, M13. M92 is visible through binoculars or a small scope.

Star magnitudes
−1 0 1 2 3 4

Variable star · Double star · Open cluster · Globular cluster · Galaxy · Planetary nebula · Diffuse nebula

Other May/June sights: The **Eta Aquarid** meteor shower peaks May 5. The meteors will appear to radiate from the constellation of Aquarius. The Eta Aquarids are better viewed from the Southern Hemisphere, however, because at northern latitudes, Aquarius doesn't rise in the east until around 2 AM.

When to use this map

Early May: 1 AM*

Late May: Midnight*

Early June: 11 PM*

Late June: Dusk

The map is also useful in early February at dawn, early March at 4 AM, and early April at 3 AM.*

*Daylight saving time

The Teapot region in Sagittarius teems with celestial wonders. Easily visible are the bright red Lagoon Nebula (M8) and a pair of sparkly blue clusters (M6 and M7), embedded in the Sagittarius Star Cloud.

Summer evenings present a particularly rich sky for observers, for that's when the Earth is turned toward the bright, star-packed nucleus of the Milky Way. In fact, the **Milky Way** is a good place to start your summer observing sessions. To get a really good view of it, though, you'll want to get out of the city and under a deep, dark sky. Only then will the dusty, white spill of stars become apparent.

Several bright stars stud the summer night sky, most of them almost directly overhead. Hold the map so that Facing South is at the bottom of the page and face the southern horizon. The first bright star to look for is **Vega**, which is directly overhead. Vega is a 0-magnitude star in the constellation of **Lyra**, the Lyre. Now look above and to the left of Vega, until you come to another bright star; this is **Deneb**, a 1st-magnitude star in the constellation of **Cygnus**, the Swan. Then extend an imaginary line down and a little to the right of Deneb. The next bright star you come to is **Altair**, also a 1st-magnitude star, in **Aquila**, the Eagle. These three bright stars form an asterism called the **Summer Triangle**, an area chock-full of celestial sights.

Go back to Deneb and draw a straight line down to the medium-bright star marking the beak of Cygnus (Deneb is the tail). This is **Albireo**, a double star. One of the summer sky's most beautiful sights, Albireo can be split with a small scope into its two component stars: one yellow, the other blue. Notice that there are several stars in that line between Deneb and Albireo. Look at the bright one nearest Deneb; it's flanked by two more reasonably bright stars. Together, all these stars take the shape of a large cross and, in fact, the group is an asterism called the **Northern Cross**.

Get out your binoculars, now, and sweep them down the Milky Way, from Cygnus through Aquila, past **Scutum**, the Shield, to **Sagittarius**, the Archer, and across to **Scorpius**, the Scorpion. Don't look for anything specific; just marvel at the abundance of stars you can see in this area. In particular, the sky around Sagittarius and the tail of Scorpius is aglow with binocular and telescopic sights.

Now go back to Sagittarius. It's a zodiacal constellation, so you'll find it along the ecliptic, which is marked on the map. Notice that on the map, the bright stars of Sagittarius look like a teapot. The **Teapot** is actually an asterism within the constellation. Scan the bright, star-filled sky immediately above the spout of the Teapot with binoculars. This is the **Sagittarius Star Cloud**; when you look here, you're looking toward the center of our galaxy. Just above the Cloud you'll find a pair of open clusters, **M23** and **M25**, as well as a globular cluster, **M22**. Also visible are several nebulas: **M17**, the **Swan**, **Omega**, or **Horseshoe Nebula**; **M20**, the very lovely **Trifid Nebula**; and **M8**, the **Lagoon Nebula**. Here, too, is the **Small Sagittarius Star Cloud (M24)**. Bring the binoculars down a bit, to near the tail of Scorpius, where you can see two more open clusters, **M6** and **M7**. A small scope will show the clusters and nebulas in more detail and clarity, but you'll want to find them with binoculars first.

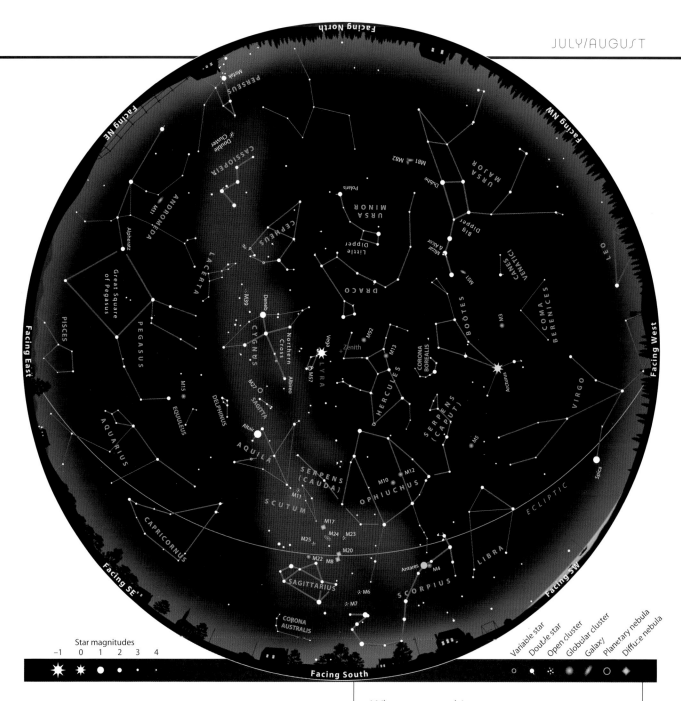

Star magnitudes
−1 0 1 2 3 4

Variable star · Double star · Open cluster · Globular cluster · Galaxy · Planetary nebula · Diffuse nebula

Other July/August sights: The **Delta Aquarid** meteor shower peaks on July 29. Like May's Eta Aquarids, the radiant is in Aquarius, but in a slightly different location. The Eta Aquarids are bits of rocky debris shed by Comet Halley, while the source of the Delta Aquarids is uncertain. One of the best meteor showers, the **Perseids**, peaks around August 12; Comet Swift-Tuttle is the source of these meteors. The radiant, in northern Perseus, rises in the northeast after midnight.

When to use this map

Early July: Midnight*
Late July: 11 PM*
Early August: 10 PM*
Late August: Dusk

The map is also useful in late April at dawn, late May at 3 AM*, and late June at 1 AM.*

*Daylight saving time

Many of summer's celestial highlights remain visible in the autumn sky. **Cygnus**, the Swan, still flies overhead, and the three bright stars that form the Summer Triangle—**Vega**, **Deneb**, and **Altair**—are high in the sky.

Look west and hold the map with Facing West at the bottom. Find Vega, the brightest of the three stars that make up the Triangle. Immediately above Vega is a fainter star. Take a look at it through binoculars, and you'll see that it's actually a pair of stars, Epsilon 1 and Epsilon 2, a double-star system. A small- to medium-size scope, at high power, will reveal a surprise: each of these stars is also a double star. This is the famous **Epsilon Lyrae**, a quadruple-star system better known as the Double-Double. To the left of Vega, at the other end of Lyra, is a favorite of stargazers, **M57**, the **Ring Nebula**. You'll need a telescope and moderate power to see the doughnut shape of this planetary nebula; look for it between the two bright end stars of Lyra.

From M57, hop up and to the left, to the lovely double star, Albireo, then keep going until you spot a pattern of four closely knit stars. This is the tiny constellation of **Sagitta**, the Arrow. Just to the right of the star marking the point of the arrow, in neighboring Vulpecula, is another planetary nebula, the **Dumbbell Nebula**, or **M27**. It's bigger and brighter than the Ring Nebula and visible in binoculars, but it can be tricky to find.

Turn the map slightly, so that Facing SW is at the bottom, then find Altair, in Aquila. Draw a line from Altair straight down to the star at the eagle's beak. Just past it, in the space between Aquila and the top star in the constellation of **Scutum**, the Shield, is **M11**, a beautiful open cluster that's visible through binoculars but better seen through a small scope. Surrounding it is the bright **Scutum Star Cloud**; after you've found M11, take a moment to sweep your binoculars through this region that's been called "the gem of the Milky Way."

Looking vaguely like an apple core at the center of this photo is the Dumbbell Nebula (M27), a telescope sight in the small constellation of Vulpecula.

Now look to the south and turn the map so Facing South is at the bottom. Less than half-way up the sky, between the horizon and the zenith, is **Capricornus**, the Sea Goat. Looking more like a sailboat than a goat, Capricornus lies along the ecliptic. Take a look at the two brightest stars in the constellation, the ones at the top of the sail, through binoculars—they're both binary stars. The upper one, **Alpha Capricorni**, is easy to split, as both stars are almost the same brightness. The lower one, **Beta**, is more challenging, as one star is much fainter than the other.

Finally, face the eastern horizon, holding the map so Facing East is at the bottom. A little more than half way up the sky, you should see four bright stars forming a slightly askew square. This is the **Great Square** in the constellation of **Pegasus**, the Winged Horse. This star pattern will come in handy later on, when you're looking for other constellations. Find the bright star in the upper-right corner of the square, then follow the fainter stars up and to the right that form a hooked line. Near the moderately bright star at the end of the line is **M15**, a compact globular cluster that's a fine sight in a small telescope.

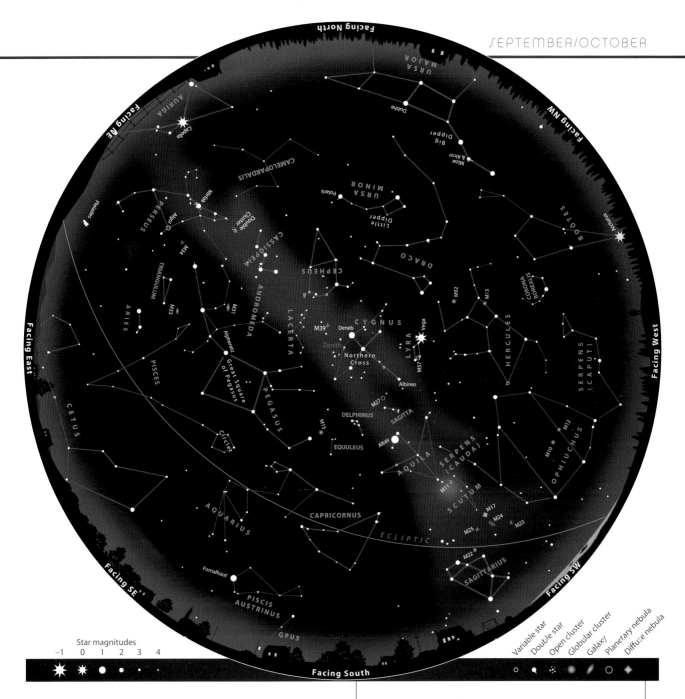

Star magnitudes
−1 0 1 2 3 4

Facing North

Facing NE

Facing NW

Facing East

Facing West

Facing SE

Facing SW

Facing South

Variable star
Double star
Open cluster
Globular cluster
Galaxy
Planetary nebula
Diffuse nebula

Other September/October sights: The **Orionid** meteor shower peaks October 22. The meteors radiate from near Betelgeuse in Orion, which rises in the eastern sky around midnight. Like the Eta Aquarids in May, the source of the Orionids is Comet Halley.

When to use this map

Early September: 11 PM*

Late September: 10 PM*

Early October: 9 PM*

Late October: Dusk

The map is also useful in late June at dawn, late July at 2 AM*, and late August at midnight.*

Daylight saving time

Characters out of Greek mythology—a queen, a maiden, a flying horse, and a hero—rule the night sky in November and December. Start the night by facing south, holding the map so that Facing South is at the bottom. Look high overhead and find the four bright stars that make up the **Great Square** of **Pegasus**. The bright star in the upper-left corner of the square (Alpheratz) and the next two bright stars that curve to the upper left of it are part of another constellation: **Andromeda**, the Chained Maiden (aka the Princess, or Daughter of Cassiopeia). Above the square and the arc of

The small, elliptical smudge in this photo is actually M31, the Andromeda Galaxy, visible in very dark skies to the naked eye.

Andromeda (you'll have to lean back a bit so you can look past the zenith) is a pattern of four bright (and one not-so-bright) stars forming a badly drawn letter W. This is the constellation of **Cassiopeia**, the Queen. Between the Maiden and her mother, at the zenith, is the Milky Way Galaxy's nearest large neighbor, the **Andromeda Galaxy**, or **M31**. If you have a really dark sky, you might be able to see Andromeda with the

naked eye as a very dim blur. Binoculars or a small telescope will show a slightly larger elongated smudge with a central glow. Far below the western (right) edge of the Great Square is the bright star **Fomalhaut**, in **Piscis Austrinus**, the Southern Fish, which is low in the southern sky.

Now turn to the east and hold the map, so that Facing East is at the bottom. Look high for Cassiopeia which, because you're looking at her from a different direction, now resembles the number 3. Just below Cassiopeia is the **Double Cluster** in the constellation of **Perseus**, the Rescuer of Andromeda. Under dark skies, the Double Cluster is visible to the naked eye as a hazy patch in the Milky Way; through binoculars or a small telescope, it becomes two distinct halos of glittering stars. A little below is **Mirfak**, the brightest star in Perseus. Mirfak is a member of, and is surrounded by, a small, sparkling group of stars known as the **Alpha Persei Association**. To the right of Mirfak is **Algol**, a variable star whose brightness fades for a few hours every 2.87 days, as one star passes in front of the other.

Several bright stars stud the eastern sky at this time of year, including **Capella**, in the constellation of **Auriga**, the Charioteer (just below Perseus) and orange **Aldebaran**, in Taurus, the Bull. These stars and their constellations are better explored during the winter months.

Finally, hold the map so Facing North is at the bottom and look for **Cepheus**, the King, to the lower left of Cassiopeia. Find the three relatively faint stars that are arranged in a straight line along the top of the constellation. The one farthest to the left is **Delta Cephei**, a pulsating variable star, whose brightness fluctuates from magnitude 3.5 to 4.3 over a short period of 5 1/3 days. Delta Cephei has a faint companion; a small telescope will "split" the pair.

While you're facing north, look down to the northern horizon. Assuming you have a clear view of the north, can you find the Big Dipper? If not, that's because you don't live far enough north for the Dipper to be circumpolar. If you're south of 40° latitude, part or all of the Dipper will disappear for a while during the autumn.

Star magnitudes
−1 0 1 2 3 4

Variable star | Double star | Open cluster | Globular cluster | Galaxy | Planetary nebula | Diffuse nebula

Facing South

Other November/December sights: The **Taurid** meteor shower, which peaks on November 3 (radiant in Taurus); the **Leonid** meteor shower, which peaks on November 19 (radiant in the Sickle of Leo); and the **Geminid** meteor shower, which peaks on December 14 (radiant in Gemini). Of the three, the Geminid shower is the best; under dark skies, you may be able to spot sixty to seventy bright meteors an hour.

When to use this map

Early November: 10 PM

Late November: 9 PM

Early December: 8 PM

Late December: 7 PM

The chart is also useful in early August at dawn, early September at 3 AM*, and early October at 1 AM.*

Daylight saving time

t may be cold outside, but the celestial sights awaiting discovery at this time of year are spectacular. Winter is when the familiar figure of **Orion**, the Hunter, makes his appearance, striding high in the southern sky. Hold the map so that Facing South is at the bottom and look about half-way up the sky. You should see the seven bright stars of Orion. The second brightest, marking the Hunter's left shoulder, is **Betelgeuse** (magnitude 0.5), a red supergiant. At Orion's right shoulder is **Bellatrix** (magnitude 1.6). Below, at Orion's right knee, is blue-white Rigel, at magnitude 0.2, while is other knee is marked by fainter **Saiph**. Midway, at Orion's waist, are the three bright 2nd-magnitude stars that make up Orion's belt. It's below the belt, in Orion's sword, that you'll find the oft-photographed and truly stunning **M42**, or **Great Orion Nebula**. While it's only a dim, fuzzy patch through binoculars, a 3- or 4-inch (75- or 100-mm) scope will reveal structure within the cloud, as well as the four hot, young stars of the **Trapezium**.

Like the Big Dipper (which is currently low in the northeast), the seven bright stars of the Hunter can be used as signposts to help you find various bright winter stars and constellations. Extending a line down through Orion's belt stars brings you to brilliant **Sirius**, in the constellation of **Canis Major**, the Big Dog. At magnitude −1.4, it's the brightest star in our sky—next to the Sun, of course. Just below (south) and slightly to the right of Sirius is **M41**, an open star cluster, visible in binoculars or a small telescope. Two more clusters, **M47** and **M46**, are just to the left (east) of Sirius. To the upper left of Sirius is the bright star **Procyon** in **Canis Minor**, the Little Dog.

Go back to Orion and draw a line through his belt, extending it to the upper right. This will bring you to the bright star **Aldebaran** in **Taurus**, the Bull, which is high in the southern sky, along with the ecliptic. Right next to it is the **Hyades**, a lovely open cluster, visible to the naked eye as an extended V. Aldebaran isn't physically part of the Hyades; the cluster is twice as far away as this reddish orange star.

Now extend the line a little past Aldebaran and you'll find one of the best-known deep-sky objects, the **Pleiades**, a bright open cluster visible to the naked eye as a group of six or seven stars. Its nickname is the Seven Sisters, but most people can only see six of them. Binoculars show the blue-white stars clearly, sparkling against a backdrop of fainter stars, while a mid-sized telescope (from a dark-sky site) may reveal wisps of the nebulosity surrounding the stars.

The Pleiades, visible to the naked eye, is a beautiful and familiar open cluster of stars.

Return to Orion and, from the middle star in his belt, extend a line straight up between Betelgeuse and Bellatrix until, near the zenith, you encounter the bright star **Capella**, in the constellation of **Auriga**, the Charioteer. A little below Capella, just above the second-brightest star in Auriga, are a pair of open star clusters, **M36** and **M38**. Just to their left is **M37**, another, larger open cluster. All are fine sights in binoculars or a small scope.

Finally, revisit the Hunter one last time. Draw a line from the middle star in his Belt, through Betelgeuse, and on to the upper left until you encounter a pair of stars. They are **Castor** and **Pollux** in **Gemini**, the Twins. We explore these stars, and the constellation, in March/April highlights.

Star magnitudes
−1 0 1 2 3 4

Variable star   Double star   Open cluster   Globular cluster   Galaxy   Planetary nebula   Diffuse nebula

Facing South

Other January/February sights: The **Quadrantid** meteor shower peaks on January 3. The radiant for this shower is in **Boötes**, the Herdsman, which is low in the northeastern sky, just below the handle of the Big Dipper, at this time of year.

When to use this map

Early January: 10 PM

Late January: 9 PM

Early February: 8 PM

Late February: Dusk

The map is also useful in early October at 5 AM*, early November at 2 AM, and early December at midnight.

*Daylight saving time

CHAPTER SEVEN
COMETS, METEORS, AND SATELLITES

COMETS

On the surface, the solar system seems a fairly predictable place. The Sun rises in the east every morning and sets in the west every evening. Stars and constellations wheel overhead, sometimes dipping below the horizon for a few months but always returning at the same time every year. The Moon cycles through its phases. Oh, we might get a transit or an eclipse now and then, but we can predict those years in advance. Nothing much changes. Which is how we prefer it—imagine the chaos if the Earth suddenly started rotating in the opposite direction!

Historically, people have preferred predictability, as well—which is why the sudden appearance of a comet in the sky gave skywatchers of old the heebie-jeebies. What were these "hairy stars," as the Greeks dubbed them? And where did they come from? Most people decided they were bad news, for comets often seemed to appear when a battle was lost, a ruler died, or the plague came calling. The first sight of one of these ghostly apparitions sent people scurrying inside behind locked doors, to avoid the "poisonous" vapors the unwelcome visitor brought with it.

Today, most of us have the opposite reaction. News of a comet, particularly a bright one, brings us out under the skies, binoculars in hand, to marvel at one of the solar system's intermittent visitors.

Comet Hale-Bopp, one of the brightest comets to come along in decades, hangs over a mountain landscape in this photo, taken April 12, 1997, when the comet was closest to Earth.

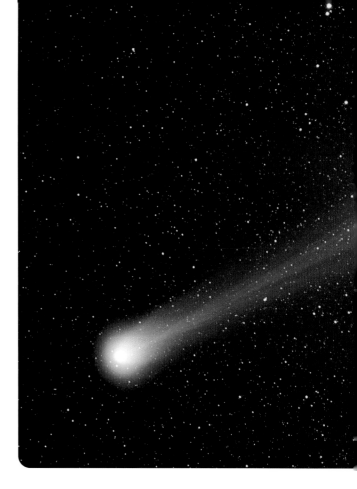

First, a Little Background

So, what are comets? Most often described as "dirty snowballs" (albeit large ones: the average comet ranges in diameter from two to ten miles, or three to sixteen kilometers), comets are balls of frozen gas, dust, and water that spend most of their time drifting in a region known as the Kuiper Belt, far beyond the orbit of Neptune. Millions of them dwell out here, and as many as a trillion reside beyond that, in a vast sphere called the Oort Cloud.

Once in a while, one of these balls, or comet *nuclei*, gets nudged out of the Belt or the Cloud and starts heading into the inner solar system, where it undergoes a dramatic transformation (rather like a caterpillar turning into a butterfly). As it nears the Sun, the surface of the icy ball begins to heat up and vaporize—that is, it turns to gas. A huge cloud of this gas (called a *coma*), sometimes reaching hundreds of thousands of miles in diameter, forms around the nucleus and is then swept back by the solar wind into a long, glowing *tail*, turning the "dirty snowball" into a thing of beauty.

Some comets, like Halley, return again and again to our skies—we refer to them as *periodic* comets. Those that return in less than 200 years are called short-period comets. Comets with longer orbital periods are called, not surprisingly, long-period comets, some of which can take tens of millions of years to complete one orbit. Short-period comets are thought to come from the Kuiper Belt and have orbits similar to the planets'; that is, they're fairly close to the plane of the solar system. Long-period comets, on the other hand, which are thought to originate in the Oort Cloud, seem to swoop into the inner solar system from every direction. A few comets, not periodic in nature, drop by just once, then snub us forever after. And

Comet Halley
Very few comets are as bright as Hale-Bopp. Not even Comet Halley, which is usually a bright comet. In 1986, when Halley last dropped by to visit, its performance was rather lackluster, and it looked more like a faint fuzzy—the type we most often see—than its usual self.

Observing Comets

When Comet Hale-Bopp visited our skies in 1997, it was something of an event. The most-observed comet since Halley's last appearance in 1986, Hale-Bopp was so bright, it was spotted two years before its closest approach to Earth. (For more on Hale-Bopp, see Famous Comets, page 101.)

Most of the comets passing through, however, are not nearly as spectacular. In fact, even Hale-Bopp wasn't as brilliant as it appears in photos—for the same reason that everything you see in the skies pales in comparison to a photograph: film is much more sensitive to light and will pick up color and detail that the human eye cannot see. Which means that most comets will appear, to the naked eye, as little more than faint, fuzzy patches in the sky. Even through binoculars, these "faint fuzzies," as they are sometimes called, are still, well . . . faint and fuzzy.

Every now and then, a "celebrity" comet like Hale-Bopp or Ikeya-Seki comes along and makes up for the pallid performance of the faint fuzzies. What makes them so special? Visible for more than a year, Hale-Bopp was bright because of its size—its nucleus was almost 25 miles (40 km) in diameter! Some comets are bright because of their proximity to the Sun or to Earth, while others throw off a lot of light-reflecting dust. Sometimes, comets are memorable for other features, such as the length of their tails. In addition to its proximity to the Sun, Ikeya-Seki also boasted one of longest tails ever to be sported by a comet: 93 million miles (150 million km)—the length of the distance between the Earth and the Sun!

Comets' tails are not always visible (see faint fuzzies, above), and no two are exactly alike. Hale-Bopp's two distinct tails—the straight, blue, gas tail and the curved, pale-yellow, dust tail—were clearly visible, while Comet Hyakutake's dust tail was very faint, which made the comet appear to have only one tail. Some comets, such as Ikeya-Seki, have long tails; others are shorter.

then there are the "Sun-grazers," Kamikaze-like comets, whose orbits take them very close—and sometimes straight into—the Sun. Ikeya-Seki was one of these. In 1965, the comet's path took it so close to the Sun, it became bright enough to be seen in daylight. When it emerged from behind the solar orb, it had broken into two pieces.

A common misconception about comets is that they streak across the sky, when in fact, with a few exceptions, comets move so slowly, you have to watch for an hour or more to see any change in their position—giving you more time to appreciate their beauty.

TAIL FIRST

When a comet orbits the Sun, its tail always faces away from the solar orb. Why? Because of the solar wind, which pushes the tail away from the Sun. On its approach to the Sun, a comet's tail streams out behind it, and the comet comes in head first. But as the comet moves away from the Sun, the tail actually leads the comet. Eventually, as the comet returns to the outer reaches of the solar system, its head and tail shrink, leaving just the icy nucleus.

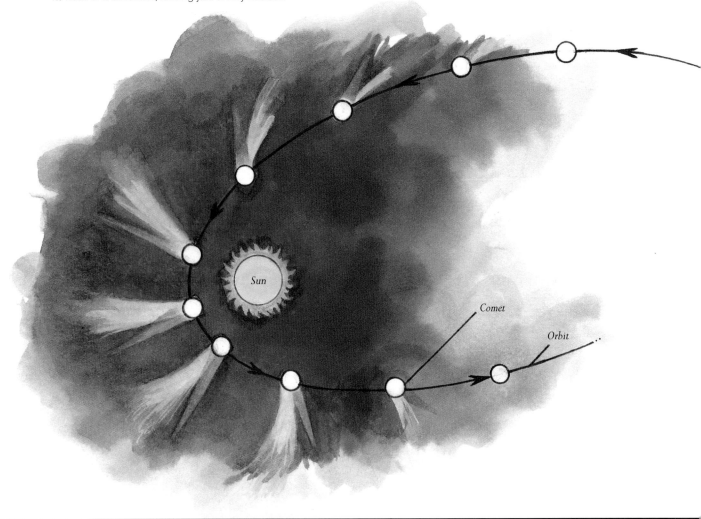

How do you know when and where to look for a comet? Unless you're one of the dedicated amateur astronomers who spend years scrutinizing the skies for the first sign of a comet (their reward is having comets they've discovered named after them), you'll probably hear about its appearance, along with where and when to look for it, from an astronomy magazine or even in the news, if the comet is bright enough. Some astronomy websites regularly note celestial events when they occur. And, since some comets—Halley, for instance, which returns every seventy-six years—are periodic, we already know when to expect them back.

FAMOUS COMETS

Some comets are more memorable than others—and not always for the best of reasons. Here are a select few.

Comet Halley   Ask anyone to name a comet and you can bet the answer will be Halley—though it's likely to be pronounced HAIL-y, rather than HAL-y (rhymes with valley), which is the correct way to say it. Comet Halley's claim to fame is two-fold: it's usually a reasonably bright comet, and it comes around every seventy-six years, so most people get a chance to see it once in their lifetime.

Halley has been coming around for a while: it was spotted as long ago as 467 BC, although it hadn't been named Halley yet. That didn't happen until after the comet's appearance in 1758–just when astronomer Edmund Halley predicted it would show up. Halley (the comet, not the astronomer) was last seen in 1986, so if you missed it and you want to see its return, you'll have to find a way to stick around until 2061.

Hale-Bopp
Comet Hale-Bopp is memorable for two reasons: its spectacular brightness and its association with the Heaven's Gate cult, which believed the comet to be hiding a spaceship.

Celestial Collision
Comet Shoemaker-Levy 9 leaves its mark—well, several marks—on Jupiter in this photograph, taken by the Hubble Space Telescope. The "bruises" were caused by fragments of the comet crashing into the planet in July 1994.

Comet Shoemaker-Levy 9   Eugene and Carolyn Shoemaker and David Levy spotted this comet on the night of March 23, 1993, their ninth comet discovery. Not a bright comet (at magnitude 14, it was invisible, unless you had a fairly large scope), Shoemaker-Levy 9 was famous for its death, rather than its appearance. When Levy and the Shoemakers discovered the comet, it was in orbit around Jupiter, captured by the giant planet's gravity, and it had broken into pieces. Spread out like a "string of pearls," as they came to be described, the twenty-one comet fragments made history when they crashed into Jupiter from July 16 through July 22, 1994, leaving a series of black "bruises" in the planet's atmosphere. Although we know that celestial bodies do smash into each other on occasion, this was the first time in history that a collision between two solar system bodies had ever been observed.

Comet Hale-Bopp   Hale-Bopp's celebrity is well-deserved; spectacularly bright and long-lived, the comet graced our skies for a full year and put on a show that hadn't been seen in decades. Unfortunately, Hale-Bopp is also remembered for more somber reasons. On March 27, 1997, when Hale-Bopp was closest to Earth, thirty-nine members of California's Heaven's Gate cult, believing that a spaceship lay in wait for them behind the comet, committed suicide. The ship, they believed, was waiting to take them "to the next level."

Comet Kohoutek   So, why is Kohoutek famous? Mostly because of what it didn't do. Every so often, usually once a decade or so, a comet is hailed as "the Comet of the Century." Kohoutek was one of these. Spotted in March 1973, more than nine months before its closest approach, the comet was predicted to be a jaw-dropper. As the hype grew, so did the anticipation. Unfortunately, when it finally showed up, it was less than spectacular. Barely visible without binoculars or a telescope, Kohoutek was a dud and is now remembered as a comet that failed to live up to expectations.

Night Lights
A pair of meteors streaks through the constellation of Orion during a Leonid meteor shower.

METEORS

You may call them shooting stars. You may call them falling stars. You may even wish upon them, if you're the romantic sort. But the sudden flashes of light you sometimes see streaking across the sky—usually just out of the corner of your eye—aren't stars at all, they're meteors.

First, A Little Background

Not only is the solar system not as predictable as you might think, it's also not very tidy. In fact, it's littered with debris: leftovers, like asteroids and the icy objects in the Kuiper Belt and Oort Cloud; bits and pieces of rock chipped off of colliding asteroids or thrown into space by objects smashing into planets and moons; and particles of comet dust.

More than 100 tons (90,000 kg) of this dust and debris enters Earth's atmosphere every day. Most of it, in the form of nearly invisible, microscopic particles, simply floats to the ground. (The dust on your book shelves? Yep—space dust.) But the larger bits, those about the size of a pea or grain of sand, don't. Instead, they burn up in the atmosphere, causing the bright streaks of light we call meteors.

Most of these streaks and flashes are *sporadic*, or random, meteors that appear on any given night; you can see up to half a dozen or more of these an hour, if the sky is clear and dark. But several times a year, the number of meteors falling over your head increases dramatically. These are meteor showers, which happen when the Earth crosses the trails of debris left behind by disintegrating comets on their journey around the Sun. Most meteor showers are associated with a particular comet: the Perseids, for instance, which occur in August, are caused by debris from Comet Swift-Tuttle. November's Leonids come courtesy of Comet Tempel-Tuttle, the Aquarids and Orionids are associated with Halley, and the Taurids with Encke. (See table on page 105, for when to watch for major meteor showers.)

Not all meteors are caused by comet dust, though. A very few are baseball-sized, or larger, chunks of rock knocked off of asteroids, and what they lack in quantity, they make up for in quality. Called *fireballs*, they blaze across the sky, leaving a glowing trail behind them. Sometimes, they even create a sonic boom. And, if they break apart noisily and spectacularly, they're called *bolides*. Asteroids can also be the cause of meteor showers. The Geminids, in December, for example, are generated by debris from Asteroid 3200, Phaethon.

METEORS, METEORITES, OR METEOROIDS?

Okay, so what's the difference between a meteor, a meteorite, and a meteoroid?

Floating throughout the solar system are leftover dust particles from passing comets and bits of debris from asteroids that have knocked into each other. These are called meteoroids. Sometimes, a meteoroid will fall into Earth's atmosphere, where it vaporizes, causing a bright flash of light, called a meteor. A piece of debris large enough to make it to the ground without burning up is called a meteorite.

Observing Meteors

You're likely to see a few random meteors during any observing session, especially if you have a dark sky. But, if you want to experience some serious meteor action, you'll want to head out during a meteor shower.

When's the best time to watch? Check out the table on the next page for meteor shower dates; you'll see they occur year-round. The Perseid meteor shower, in August, is considered the best shower; you'll not only see more meteors per hour, you'll find the weather a little more pleasant than in November and December, when the Leonids or Geminids occur.

You'll also want to find out what the Moon is doing. If it's within a few days of full phase, the sky will be too bright to see much of anything. The best meteor observing takes place when the Moon is between new and first quarter—when it casts less light and sets before midnight. As for the best time of night to watch, be prepared to stay up late. Meteor numbers usually peak in the early morning hours; that is, between 1 AM and dawn.

Make yourself comfortable. Get out that lounge chair, so you can lean back to get a wide view of the sky. It can become really frustrating to consistently hear "Oh, wow!" when you were looking in the wrong direction. For the same reason, you'll want to forego the binoculars—their field of view is much too small. Dress warmly. It can get cold when you're not moving around much, even on summer evenings. And be sure to bring the usual accessories: a red-light flashlight, your observing log, and a thermos full of something hot!

The Radiant

You may notice, while watching a meteor shower, that the meteors seem to originate from a certain point in the sky. This point is called the *radiant*. In this photo, meteors streak outward from their radiant in the constellation Leo. The radiant gives a meteor shower its name, which is why this one is called the Leonid meteor shower. It also tells you in which direction to look for meteors during a shower—in the case of the Leonids, in the direction of Leo. (See table on next page for radiants of the major annual showers.)

MAJOR METEOR SHOWERS

Dates given for the showers indicate early-morning observing—from 1 AM to dawn.

Month	Shower	Peaks	Radiant
January	Quadrantids*	Jan 3	Boötes
April	Lyrids	Apr 22	Lyra
May	Eta Aquarids	May 5	Aquarius
July	Delta Aquarids	July 29	Aquarius
August	Perseids	Aug 12	Perseus
October	Orionids	Oct 22	Orion
November	Taurids	Nov 3	Taurus
	Leonids	Nov 19	Leo
December	Geminids	Dec 14	Gemini

Why is Boötes the radiant for the Quadrantids? Because the shower was named for a constellation that is no longer officially recognized: Quadrans, the Quadrant. Bootes is now the constellation nearest to the radiant.

Satellites and Other Man-Made Moving Things

Once you start observing, it won't be long before you'll notice, one night, a bright dot of light sailing by overhead. "What the heck is that?" you wonder. A plane? A UFO?

Well, it could be, but most likely you're seeing a satellite. Thousands of them—for communications, weather, military, astronomical, navigational, and earth-resources purposes—orbit the Earth on a regular basis. Thousands more objects orbit along with them, in the form of space junk: dead rockets, hatch covers, bolts, camera lenses, and other pieces of garbage left behind by our various forays into space. Like the Moon, they have no light of their own; they shine because sunlight bounces off the satellite's metallic parts. In fact, if you study one of these traveling dots with a pair of binoculars and discover that it does have lights, you're probably looking at a high-flying airplane.

Some satellites, like the International Space Station (ISS) and the space shuttle, when it's in orbit, are bright enough to see from the city. Others are much dimmer and require a dark sky. The best time to watch for satellites is in late spring and early summer about an hour or so after twilight ends. (Outside of those times, the Earth's shadow gets in the way.) Several websites, such as *www.heavens-above.com* and *www.satobs.org/satintro.html*, offer satellite-tracking services, so you can work out when one of those dots of light will pass overhead and whether it's the ISS, the Hubble Space Telescope, or a regular satellite (see Resources, page 150).

Iridium Flare

Floating above the Earth, like an army of miniature spacecraft out of a *Star Wars* movie, is a fleet of communications satellites launched by a satellite cell-phone company called Iridium LLC. Since their launch, they have generated a great deal of interest for amateur astronomers. Why? Because when one of theses satellites is angled just so, sunlight bounces off its extremely shiny, door-sized antenna arrays, causing a flare that lasts for only a few seconds but can be brighter than the planet Venus. Iridium flares are predictable; check the Resources section for websites that list when they are visible in your area.

PROJECTS

○ **PROJECT 1: Observe a Comet**

Although periodic comets do visit our skies on a regular basis, they're usually faint and difficult to find. You may want to start comet observing when you hear of a bright visitor. When a comet does come around, observe it as often as you can and draw what you see in your observing log. Can you see the comet's tail? How bright is it? How long is it visible? How does its position change over time? Observe the comet with the naked eye and through binoculars and/or a small telescope.

○ **PROJECT 2: Observe a Comet's Motion against the Background of Stars**

With a telescope, observe a comet's motion over the course of an evening. Draw its position relative to some nearby stars (or plot it on a star map), then go out regularly over a few hours and plot its motion. Does it move fast or slowly against the background of stars? If the comet is very slow-moving, you may have to repeat this procedure for several days before the comet's motion becomes really noticeable.

○ **PROJECT 3: Meteor Shower Count**

Check the table on page 105, to find out when the next meteor shower occurs (you may want to wait for a bigger shower, or one that occurs in favorable weather—the Perseids are a good one to start with). Remember, showers generally peak after midnight, so you may want to wait until near midnight to go out. Make yourself comfortable and be prepared for a long night. Once you're settled, count the number of meteors you see over the course of the shower. Note any particularly bright ones. Then note the direction from which they seem to be coming—the radiant. Note, too, any sporadic meteors you see during the shower.

○ **PROJECT 4: Spotting Satellites**

Check a satellite observing website (see Resources) to find out what satellites may be passing over your neighborhood and when, then see whether you can identify any of them. See whether you can spot the International Space Station (ISS) as it passes overhead.

CHAPTER
EIGHT
ECLIPSES

Like comets, eclipses were unwelcome occurrences in the old days. The Sun and the Moon were worshipped and revered, and if their faces darkened unexpectedly, it could only mean that the Gods were angry about something. (Unless you were Chinese, and then it meant that a dragon was swallowing the Sun, or German, in which case the Sun and the Moon were hidden because they were off canoodling with each other.)

Today, people travel thousands of miles to out-of-the-way places (Antarctica, Libya) to see a total solar eclipse that might last a minute—if it isn't clouded out. If you've never seen an eclipse, you might think they're crazy. If you have, then you know that witnessing an eclipse is an unforgettable experience, one that no photograph or page of purple prose can ever capture.

Total Eclipse of the Sun
The bright, white corona streams out from the black disk of the Sun in this photo of a total eclipse, taken in 1979 from Manitoba, Canada.

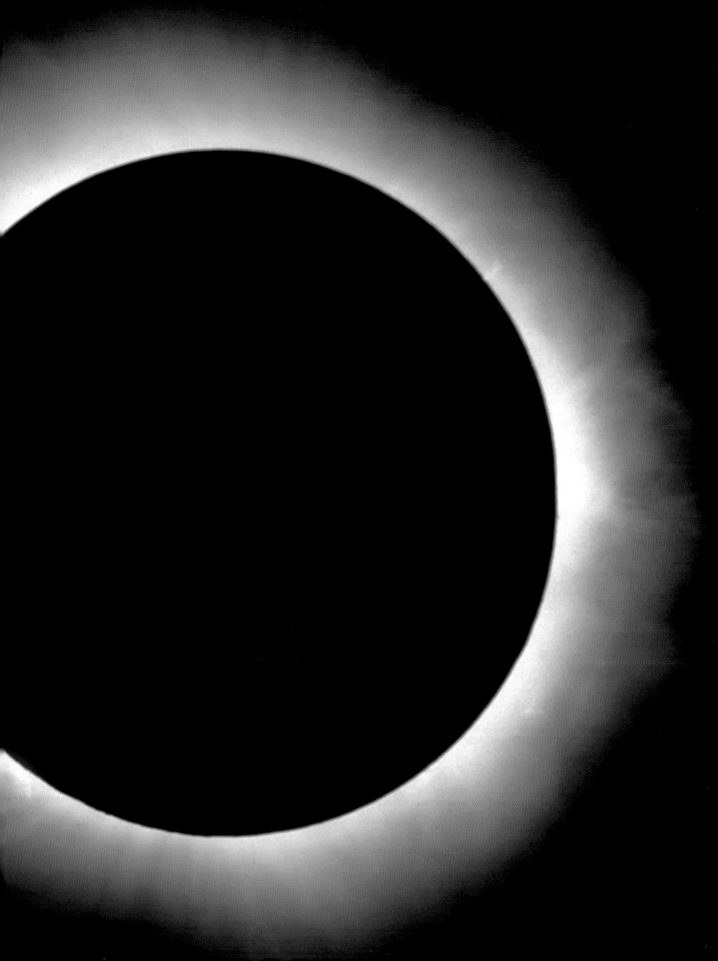

First, a Little Background

If you've read Chapter Two, you'll know that, as the Earth orbits the Sun, the Moon orbits the Earth—which means that once in a while, the Moon gets in the way and blocks our view of the Sun (causing a *solar eclipse*) or the Earth gets in the way and keeps most of the light of the Sun from reaching the Moon (causing a *lunar eclipse*).

Why doesn't this happen every month? Because the Earth, Moon, and Sun have to be exactly aligned in space for an eclipse to occur. And usually they're not. The Moon's orbit is actually tilted to the plane of the Earth's orbit around the Sun (the ecliptic) by about 5°. (Imagine two hoops, one slightly angled to the other.) The Moon moves along its angled orbit, sometimes as much as 5° above or 5° below the orbit of the Earth—which means that, during its monthly cycle around our planet, the Moon is usually too high or too low to pass exactly in front of the Sun or through Earth's shadow. Twice a month, however, the Moon crosses the ecliptic, at places called nodes, and twice a year, the nodes line up with the Sun in such a way that an eclipse is possible.

Solar Eclipses

You may be wondering how an object as small as the Moon could completely cover the disk of an object the size of the Sun. Geometry, my dear Watson, as Sherlock Holmes might have said. Simple geometry. The Sun is 400 times the diameter of the Moon, yes. But the Moon is 400 hundred times closer to the Earth than the Sun—which is the perfect formula for an eclipse, as long as the three celestial bodies are exactly aligned in space.

When that happens, the tip of the Moon's cone-shaped shadow hits a small point on the Earth. Anyone living within that area—called the *umbra*—experiences a *total eclipse*. Those who live in the *penumbra*, the area around the umbra, where the Sun is not completely obscured and the shadow is more diffuse, will see a *partial eclipse*. (See illustration.)

Of course, neither the Moon nor the Earth are standing still while all this is happening, which is why you have what's called a *path of totality*. This is the path the umbra moves along as the Moon travels through its orbit. Although the path is thousands of miles long, it's narrow, and the umbral shadow moves along it quickly; total eclipses last from a few seconds to a maximum of seven and a half minutes.

IT'S ALL ABOUT SHADOWS

For a total eclipse of the Sun to occur, the Moon, Sun, and Earth must all be in perfect alignment. When that happens, the Moon comes between the Sun and Earth and blocks the Sun's light, casting a shadow on the Earth. Those living in the area of the umbra see a total eclipse; those in the penumbra see a partial eclipse.

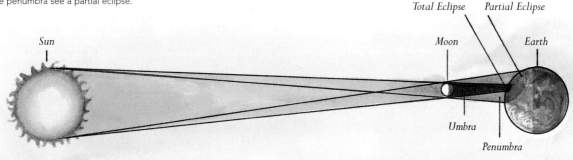

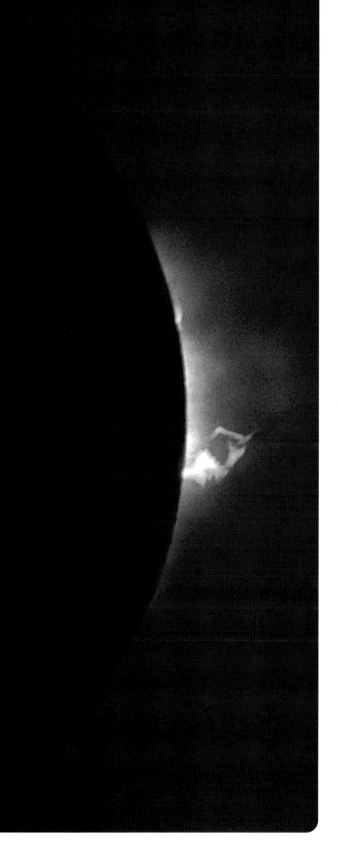

What Happens during a Solar Eclipse?

While *totality* (the time when the Sun's face is completely hidden) only lasts a moment or two, an eclipse from beginning to end can take about two hours. Astronomers have for some time been able to predict—down to the second—when and where eclipses will occur many years down the road. Which is why you'll see crowds of eclipse enthusiasts gathering along the path of totality, sometimes elbow to elbow and jockeying for position, hours before the event occurs. There's a kind of breathless anticipation as the appointed time approaches and the Moon sidles ever closer to the Sun.

And then it happens: an ever-so-small nick appears in the Sun, as the Moon takes its first bite out of the solar orb. This is *first contact*, and it's usually accompanied by a rousing cheer from the onlookers. During the next hour, the Moon slowly slides over the face of the Sun, until, at about fifteen minutes before totality, you notice that the western sky is a perceptibly deeper blue than the eastern sky. The air feels a little cooler, and the surrounding landscape seems just a little darker. As the solar crescent shrinks, bright stars and planets begin to appear in the ever-deepening sky.

Things happen quickly after this. About one or two minutes before totality, you may see the Moon's shadow sweep toward you, like a tidal wave of darkness. Up in the sky, as the final sliver of Sun is about to be swallowed up, a necklace of bright dots appears—*Baily's Beads*, caused by the last rays of the Sun shining through the valleys on the limb of the Moon. An instant before the Sun disappears, the *diamond ring* appears—a final bright bead of light tethered to a ring of chromosphere. And then the Sun is gone: *second contact*.

Prominent Prominence

A spectacular prominence leaps from the surface of the eclipsed Sun. Unless your telescope is equipped with an H-alpha filter, eclipses are your only opportunity to see solar features like this.

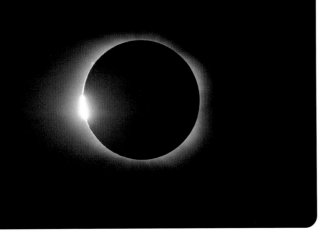

Diamond in the Sky

The bright gleam of the "diamond" ring is the last gasp of sunlight visible before the Sun's face is completely darkened by the Moon and the first gleam of light seen as the Moon slides off the face of the Sun.

In place of the Sun is a black disk surrounded by a halo of light stretching out into space. This is the corona, normally invisible to us. Visible, too, are the bright-red *prominences*, like flames from a forest fire, licking the edge of the Sun. Around you, other interesting things are occurring. In the deep twilight,

birds have gone to roost, animals become confused and disoriented, flowers draw up their petals.

All too soon, totality ends—*third contact*—and everything happens in reverse: first, the diamond ring, now on the other side of the Sun, then Baily's Beads and a gradual brightening of the landscape and sky, until *fourth contact*, when the last sliver of Moon falls away, and the eclipse is over.

Partial and Annular Eclipses

Not all eclipses are total. In fact, most of them aren't. Sometimes, the Moon obscures only part of the Sun as it passes by, in what's called a *partial eclipse*. Partial solar eclipses occur when the Moon and Sun aren't in perfect alignment: the Moon passes either above or below the center of the Sun and only covers part of the solar disk.

At other times, the Moon will slide across the center of the Sun but not quite cover it, leaving a bright ring of sunlight around the dark disk of the Moon. This is an *annular eclipse*. In an annular eclipse, the Earth, Moon, and Sun do align in space, but the Moon is too far from the Earth, and/or the Earth is too close to the Sun, for the Moon to completely cover the Sun's disk. This happens because the orbits of the Earth around the Sun and the Moon around the Earth are not circular but elliptical, which means their distance from each other varies slightly throughout the year.

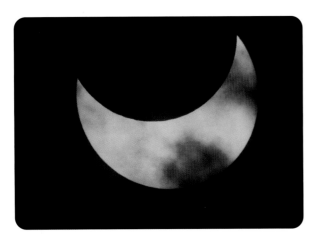

Partial Eclipse

A partial eclipse occurs when the Moon isn't quite in the right position to cover the entire face of the Sun and passes only in front of part of it. None of the spectacular phenomena you see during a total eclipse occurs during a partial eclipse.

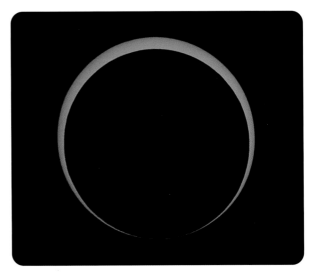

Annular Eclipse

Annular eclipses occur when the Moon's apparent size is not quite large enough to cover the entire disk of the Sun. Annulars, while not as spectacular as total eclipses, can be quite beautiful and worth traveling to see.

Viewing a Solar Eclipse Safely

The wonderful thing about a total solar eclipse is that you don't need a telescope or binoculars to enjoy it. In fact, some people prefer to experience it with the unaided eye, instead of seeing it through the narrow window of an eyepiece. On the other hand, binoculars or a telescope can reveal details in the prominences and corona that you can't see with the unaided eye.

Regardless of how you choose to view an eclipse (total or partial, but especially partial) *you must always use a solar filter!* Follow the same rules that apply to observing a non-eclipsed Sun (see Chapter Four) and protect your eyes. You can observe the eclipse without protection during totality, but be sure to put your protective glasses and filters back on before the Sun reappears. Even the briefest flash of sunlight can damage your eyes. Novices might want to stay close to more experienced observers, who will know when it is, and isn't, safe to observe the Sun without a filter.

If you're planning to take photos of the eclipse, you'll want to be sure to buy (or make) a solar filter for your camera to use during the partial phases. (Remove the filter during totality or you'll wind up with photos of nothing but black sky.) For more on photographing eclipses and other celestial events, see Chapter Eleven.

Binocular Viewing

If you're using binoculars to watch the partial phases of a solar eclipse, fit solar filters over the objective lenses. Don't forget to take them off during totality.

Chasing Totality

Although total solar eclipses aren't rare, they rarely happen where you are. In fact, the chances of seeing a total eclipse from your backyard are one in 375.

Once you've experienced one, however, you run the risk of becoming one of the many amateur astronomers who spend most of their life's savings and all their vacation days traveling around the world to see them. These are the "eclipse chasers," and many of them have see several eclipses in their lifetime, from countries all over the globe—as well as from the air and the middle of the ocean. The Appendix lists upcoming eclipses up to the year 2015. If one isn't occurring in your neighborhood, start planning your eclipse trip now, and think about signing up with a travel company specializing in astro-travel.

Practicing Safe Sun

Always protect your eyes when viewing a solar eclipse! Although it's safe to look at the Sun *during* totality, be sure to use a solar filter *before* and *after* totality. All it takes is a sliver of brilliant sunlight hitting your eyes to cause serious damage. If you're not using a telescope of binoculars, use a number 14 welder's plate, available at hardware stores.

Lunar Eclipses

Eclipse chasers will wax rhapsodic about solar eclipses. Lunar eclipses, on the other hand, while beautiful, don't engender quite the same enthusiasm. Nor do amateur astronomers travel around the world to see them. Part of the reason is that we see total eclipses of the Moon more often—despite the fact that they actually happen less frequently than total eclipses of the Sun. How can this be? Because when a total eclipse of the Sun occurs, it's seen by a very small percentage of the population—those in the path of totality. (See previous page on the chances of seeing an eclipse from your backyard.) When a total eclipse of the Moon occurs, about every two or three years, everyone on the night side of the Earth sees at least some part of totality, weather permitting.

Lunar eclipses occur when the full Moon travels into the Earth's shadow (see illustration). As the dark shadow,

called the *umbra*, passes across the lunar surface, the Moon's bright, white light gradually diminishes, until, at totality, it becomes a copper-colored to dull-red disk. (How dark it becomes depends on the weather conditions and how much dust and smog are in the Earth's atmosphere.)

Why doesn't it disappear altogether? Because some of the Sun's light is bent as it passes through the Earth's atmosphere and falls onto the Moon. Unlike solar eclipses, in which totality lasts for only a few moments, totality in a lunar eclipse can be admired for up to an hour and forty minutes. The whole event, from beginning (when the umbra first touches the Moon) to end (when the umbra makes its last contact with the lunar orb), can last almost four hours.

When only part of the full Moon moves into the Earth's shadow, we see a partial lunar eclipse.

Red Moon
With little sunlight to reflect, the face of the Moon turns a deep red, as in this photo of an eclipsed Moon.

SHADOWS AND LIGHT

A lunar eclipse occurs when the Moon passes into the shadow created by the Earth. As with solar eclipses, all three celestial orbs have to be in perfect alignment for a total lunar eclipse to occur.

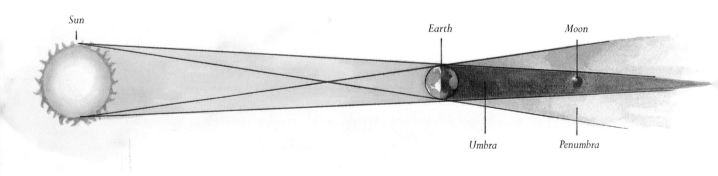

Sun

Earth   Moon

Umbra   Penumbra

Moonrise Eclipse
A partially eclipsed Moon rises over the horizon.

PROJECTS

⭕ PROJECT 1: Observe a Partial Solar Eclipse

The next time a partial solar eclipse occurs in your neighborhood, get yourself a good solar filter and go out and observe it with the unaided eye and through binoculars or a scope. Note how the Moon moves across the face of the Sun. Does it cover any sunspots?

⭕ PROJECT 2: Observe an Annular Eclipse

Annular eclipses are a little harder to come by than partials, but if you find yourself in a position to see an annular, pull out those filters and observe it. Notice what happens around you as the Moon slides in front of the Sun. Does the temperature drop? How dark does it get? Is the sky dark enough to see any bright planets? Does the landscape look odd?

⭕ PROJECT 3: Observe a Total Solar Eclipse

This is the epitome of all celestial experiences. If you're lucky enough to be in the right place at the right time to see a total eclipse (or if you've traveled to be there), try to notice what's happening around you. The effects should be the same as for the annular, right up to totality. At that point, you'll want to be looking at the eclipsed Sun. Can you see the corona? What shape is it? Using binoculars, note any promi-nences. At second and third contact, note the diamond ring. Can you see Baily's Beads?

⭕ PROJECT 4: Observe a Lunar Eclipse

The next time there's a lunar eclipse, observe it through binoculars or a small telescope during the partial phases. You'll see the shadow pass over craters. Does the edge of the Earth's shadow look sharp or fuzzy? Can you tell when the umbra first touches or last leaves the lunar disk? How bright or dark does the Moon get during totality?

Waves of green light ripple
across the northern skies,
in this photo of curtain aurora.
Just to the right of center,
you can pick out the stars
of the Big Dipper.

CHAPTER NINE
AURORAS

f you're lucky enough to live in Norway or Alaska or Scotland or any other country north of 50° N latitude, you'll be familiar with the spectacular light show known as the *aurora borealis*— or *aurora australis*, as those living at southern latitudes (south of 50° S) call it. You'll know what it's like to be riveted to the spot as shimmering curtains of ghostly green and white, now tinged with red, now rippling and snaking from right to left, perform an iridescent celestial dance above your head, sometimes for hours, sometimes for a few fleeting moments, before they fade to black.

Coronal auroras, such as this one, are less frequently seen than other types of auroral displays. Although the rays seem to emanate from a central point, they are really parallel to each other. The effect is the same as looking at railroad tracks as they converge in the distance.

What you may not know is what causes the aurora (and if there's a top ten list of frequently asked astronomy questions, this would be on it, near the top). It is not, as many people erroneously believe, caused by sunlight reflecting off polar ice or ice crystals in the air. It *is* caused by the Sun, when charged particles in the solar wind collide with atoms and molecules in the Earth's upper atmosphere, causing them to glow. The particles are drawn along the Earth's magnetic field into auroral ovals that are centered over the northern and southern magnetic poles (see illustration, opposite). People living in countries beneath those ovals are lucky enough to see the aurora fairly regularly (though it's not always a spectacular sight). Those who don't just have to wait until there's a lot of activity on the Sun—when it breaks out in a vigorous case of sunspots, for example, or ejects a huge solar flare. During these times, the aurora can be particularly breathtaking, and its glow often spreads to latitudes it doesn't normally reach. The downside to a spectacular auroral show, however, is that all this activity can

A Saturn Aurora

Earth isn't the only planet with auroras. The Hubble Space Telescope captured this photo of Saturn and its auroral ovals, in ultraviolet light. Auroras have been also been discovered on Jupiter.

wreak havoc on satellite, power, and communications networks. So, while you may be dying to share the news of your rare auroral viewing experience with everyone, you may not be able to get your cell phone to work.

Not all auroral displays are alike. While you'll often see them as a curtain of rippling light, they can also be arced or rayed or nothing more than a faint glow in the sky. Less common are coronal auroras, when you'll see streaks of light emanating from a point directly overhead, seemingly close enough to touch. They're not, though; the aurora is way up there, most commonly in a range of about 60 to 120 miles (90 to 190 km) above the Earth.

Although green is the most common color, the aurora can also be a brilliant red or tinged with blue and violet, depending on which of the atmospheric gases is interacting with the particles in the solar wind. Oxygen at low altitudes, for example, glows green (although at high altitudes it glows red). The blue and violet colors come courtesy of nitrogen.

The Aurora from Space

This photo of the aurora australis, or southern lights, was taken from the Space Shuttle. Note how the rays hover high above the clouds, in the Earth's upper atmosphere.

MAGNETIC ATTRACTION

Remember the school experiment you performed with a bar magnet and iron filings? You placed the magnet in the pile of filings and they scuttled into neat lines arcing out from the poles. Well, Earth, with its iron and molten-metal core, is just like that magnet. Lines of magnetism radiate from each of its magnetic poles. These lines, called Van Allen Belts, are what capture the charged particles of the solar wind and channel them to the poles, where they form the auroral ovals.

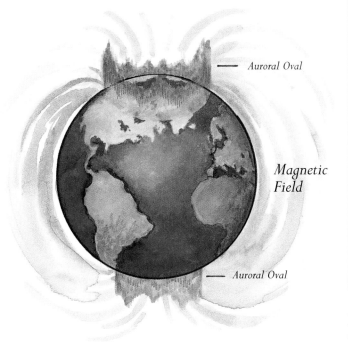

A bright ray aurora reddens the spring sky over this house in northern Alberta, Canada. Although the reason for it is not absolutely clear, March, April, September, and October are when the aurora seems to be most vivid (on a regular basis, that is—solar systems still generate the best displays, but they are unpredictable).

PROJECT

○ PROJECT 1: Observe the Aurora

If you're lucky enough to live in under those auroral ovals, this project should be easy for you. If not, you may have to travel to see an aurora or wait for the Sun to become particularly active. When you do have occasion to see an auroral display, by all means, go outside and observe it. Can you identify its type: ray, coronal, arc? What colors are visible? Make notes in your observing log.

CHAPTER TEN
ADDING OPTICS

The wonderful thing about stargazing is that it doesn't have to cost a lot of money. In fact, it doesn't have to cost anything at all. Astronomers studied the sky for thousands of years before the telescope came along—and they learned a great deal about it in the process. There's plenty to see up there with the naked eye. But human nature being what it is, eventually you—like Galileo—are going to want to see the wonders of the universe up close.

BINOCULARS

Observing with binoculars opens up a whole new world. Put binoculars in front of your eyes, and that star in the Big Dipper becomes a double star, the smudge just below Orion's belt is revealed as a nebula, and the bright speck that is Jupiter becomes a disk and four tiny moons. Aim them at the Moon, and you'll see craters and mountain ranges; aim them (filtered!) at the Sun, and you can see sunspots. Uranus and Neptune become targets, as do star clusters and even galaxies.

Essentially a joined pair of small telescopes, binoculars make faint objects brighter and small objects larger. They can turn a 3,000-star sky into a 10,000-star sky. And you probably already have a pair sitting in a closet somewhere, ones that you use for bird watching or checking out the lead guitarist from the nose-bleed seats.

Binoculars have all sorts of advantages over telescopes, especially if you're a beginner. They're easily portable, for one thing, and you can get a decent pair for about $100—much less than what you'd pay for a good telescope. (See page 123 for more on buying binoculars.) Binoculars have a greater field of view than a scope; that is, you can see a larger area of sky when you look through them, which makes it easier to find objects up there. And the objects will be right side up. (A telescope has a very small field of view, plus you're dealing with an image that is upside-down, reversed, or sometimes both!) Lastly, you're using both eyes to observe, which means you are more relaxed, and when you're more relaxed, you see more.

Binocular Basics

If you already have a pair of binoculars, take a look at them. Written somewhere on them (usually at the eyepiece end) is a pair of numbers, separated by an X; it'll be something like 7X35 (spoken as seven by thirty-five). That first number is the magnification, or power, in this case, seven. This means that whatever you're looking at will be magnified seven times. The second number indicates the diameter of the objective lens (the larger end of the binoculars), in this case, 35 millimeters. The lens is what gathers light and makes an image brighter, so the larger the lens, the more light it gathers, making faint objects easier to see.

If 7X35 binoculars are what you have, great, use them. They will certainly be an improvement over the naked eye. But, for astronomy, 7X50, 8X40, or 10X50 binoculars are a better choice. Here's why. Most 7X35 binoculars are designed to be used for hiking, bird watching, or watching the game—you'll probably be carrying them around for a few hours at a time. They're small, light, and convenient. The 35-mm objective lenses don't gather much light, but if you're bird watching, this isn't critical.

Although binoculars come in a wide range of sizes—from compact and lightweight to giant, oversized ones bigger than some small telescopes—not all of them are ideal for stargazing.

When you're looking at a faint star millions of light-years away, however, light-gathering ability is critical. Compare the 7X35s to a pair of 7X50s, for example. Even though the magnification is the same—both magnify an image seven times—objects seen through the 7X50s will appear much brighter than those seen with the 7X35s, because the larger lenses gather more light. And that extra light-gathering ability means that stars too faint to be seen through the 7X35s will be visible in the 7X50s. So you see more stars.

Why not use binoculars with even larger lenses? Monster-size binoculars (up to 150 mm!) are available—for a hefty price. But they're heavy. Unless you've been lifting 300-pound weights at the gym every morning, you'll find your arms turning rubbery trying to hold up binoculars with lenses larger than 50 mm for very long. Stick with a midsize pair to begin with, and reassess your needs once you've been stargazing for a while.

More is not necessarily better when it comes to magnification, either. Yes, Jupiter will appear larger in 10X50 binoculars than in 7X50s, but your field of view will be smaller. In other words, the amount of sky visible through 10X50s is less than 7X50s. Take the Hyades star cluster, for example. It's a perfect binocular object, but 10X50s won't be able to show you the entire cluster in one glance. That small viewing portal also makes finding objects much trickier.

Holding Them Steady

If there's a downside to binoculars, it's that, no matter how hard you try, it's difficult to keep them from shaking—even just a little. So, why does this matter? Because your shaking causes the object you're looking at to shake, too, which makes it that much harder to observe. There are ways to minimize the tremors, however.

Use binoculars with lower power. High-power binoculars magnify even the slightest amount of trembling. That's why experienced stargazers will recommend 7X, 8X or, at most, 10X binoculars—they're a good compromise between magnification and a steady view.

Lean against a wall, or rest your binoculars on a fence or rail. If you're using a lounge chair to observe, you can rest them

The larger the binoculars, the harder it is to hold them steady. One of the best ways to get a rock-solid view? Attach your binoculars to a tripod. A simple, L-shaped adapter to attach binoculars to a tripod is available for less than $20 (£10) from most camera stores; a binocular mount specially designed for astronomical use will cost considerably more. Either can help make a huge difference in your viewing experience.

against your brow bones as you lay back. In a chair, try resting your elbows on the chair arms.

Another option is to put the binoculars on a tripod, and if you're using large, heavy binoculars, a tripod is a must. But even smaller ones will benefit from being mounted on a stable, shake-free base. You could also try attaching your binoculars to a monopod (photographers often use these). Anything that stabilizes them will be an improvement over holding them by hand.

Image-stabilized binoculars are also a good way to go. These have a small button that, when pushed, counteracts any tremors. You can use these on the deck of a heaving ship, if you want, and the image will remain steady. One caveat: they cost a good deal more than regular binoculars. However, if you can afford them, they will make a huge difference—regardless of what you're observing.

Buying Binoculars

In the market for binoculars? Whether buying your first or your fourth pair, you should know what to look for. Do some homework before you buy (see Resources for reputable manufacturers), and don't go for the first pair you see. You don't have to spend a lot of money—some lesser-priced binoculars offer decent optics and quality. But before you lay any cash on the counter, check them out. Here's how.

1. Start by checking out the workmanship. Gently turn them over in your hand. If anything rattles or seems loose, reject them. Twist the barrels, too, moving them back and forth, to see if the hinge is stiff, jerky or too loose. You want the hinge to move smoothly. If you're considering a pair of used binoculars—and some good ones can be had—look for damage: reject any with dents and bumps or chipped, scratched, dirty or mildewed lenses.

2. Check the optical coatings. Hold the binoculars and look at the objective lenses. They should look dark, not bright and reflective. Darker lenses have antireflective coatings that allow more light into the lens, instead of reflecting it back. (Some have coated optics inside, as well.) If you can clearly see your face in the lenses, put them back on the shelf and move on.

3. Holding the binoculars at arm's length, aim them against a bright background and look at the eyepieces. You'll see a pair of small bright discs, where the light is passing through them. These are called the exit pupils. These should be uniformly round, not squared off. Squared-off exit pupils indicate lesser quality or undersized internal prisms, which won't let all the light through.

4. Now hold the binoculars up to your eyes and try focusing them. Depending on the model, there should either be a focus knob in the center and a focus ring on one eyepiece, or a focus ring on both eyepieces. If it's a center-knob focus, aim the binoculars at an object about 20 feet (6 m) away, then turn the center knob until the object in the left eyepiece is sharp and clear. Turn the ring on the right eyepiece to focus the image seen with your right eye. If the binoculars have individual focus rings, turn each until the object is sharp when seen with both eyes.

5. Relax your eyes and just look through the eyepieces for a minute or two. Do you feel dizzy or slightly nauseated? Does something seem off to you? Do you feel better when you look away? If you answered yes to any of these questions, chances are, the binoculars are out of alignment. Put them in the rejected category.

6. The last test involves taking the binoculars home and testing their performance under the stars, so be sure you can exchange or return them if they're not up to scratch. Stars should look sharp and come to points, and there shouldn't be a lot of fuzziness around the edges. (You'll find some edge-of-field distortion in all but the most expensive glasses; just be sure it's minimal.) If either of these applies, return them.

Binoculars are easy to take anywhere, and you can use them for nonastronomical viewing, too.

You're never too young to take your first look through a scope.

TELESCOPES

So, it's finally time to invest in a telescope. Where do you begin? It's a good question. Faced with a bewildering array of types, sizes, and price tags, it's easy to become confused.

First tip: don't go for the most expensive scope you can find. Likewise, don't go for the cheapest. While you can find a decent starter scope for less than you might expect to pay, you'll first need to learn the difference between a low-priced good scope and a low-priced scope that will cause you nothing but frustration. How do you do that? By doing research. Read the rest of this chapter; check out telescope reviews online, in astronomy magazines, and in the annual telescope-buyer's guide in *SkyWatch* magazine; go to star parties and ask seasoned stargazers for advice; and try out as many scopes as you can,

Your first scope doesn't need to be large or fancy, but it does need to be a quality instrument. And if you get hooked on stargazing, your first scope probably won't be your last.

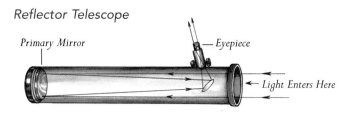

Reflector Telescope

Primary Mirror — Eyepiece

← Light Enters Here

until you feel comfortable enough with the terminology and specifications to choose the scope that's right for you.

Do not walk into the camera department of your local department store and buy the scope with the flashiest packaging. It's likely to be little better than junk, and you'll be left frustrated, disappointed, and possibly turned off of stargazing altogether.

Types of Telescopes

Optical technology has come a long way since Galileo held a telescope up to his eye. A standard pair of modern binoculars will reveal more celestial sights than any seventeenth-century astronomer ever saw through his simple spyglass. The bad news? Choosing a scope is much more complicated than it used to be, especially for first-time buyers. Here's a primer.

Telescopes fall into three general categories: *refractors, reflectors,* and *catadioptrics,* also known as compound telescopes (Schmidt-Cassegrain or Maksutov-Cassegrain for example). These three basic types of telescopes differ in the way they collect light and send it to your eye: refractors use a lens; reflectors use mirrors; and catadioptrics ("cats") use a combination of lenses and mirrors (see illustration).

Refractors   The simplest type of telescope (and the one Galileo used), a refractor has an objective lens mounted at one end of the telescope to collect light from a distant object and send it down the tube, where an eyepiece magnifies the focused image.

Reflectors   Isaac Newton invented the reflecting telescope in 1668. Reflectors use mirrors instead of a lens to gather starlight. In a classic Newtonian reflector, parallel rays of light enter the open tube at one end and are collected by a concave mirror (called the primary) at the other end. A cone of light is then bounced back up the tube to a small, flat mirror (called the secondary). Mounted on a 45° angle, the secondary mirror redirects the cone of light to a magnifying eyepiece mounted on the side of the tube.

Catadioptric Telescope

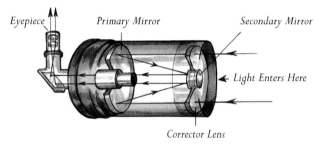

Eyepiece   Primary Mirror   Secondary Mirror

← Light Enters Here

Corrector Lens

Catadioptric Telescopes   The most complex type of telescope, a "cat" uses a combination of lenses and mirrors. Light passes through a thin corrector lens at the front of the tube on its way to the primary mirror at the other end. The primary reflects the cone of light up the tube to the secondary mirror, which then sends it back down the tube and through a small hole in the center of the primary. The light is magnified by an eyepiece behind the mirror.

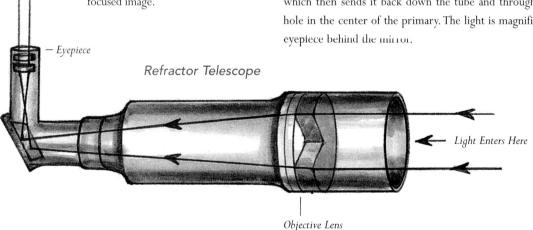

— Eyepiece

Refractor Telescope

← Light Enters Here

Objective Lens

Buying a Telescope

If price isn't the primary consideration when buying your first scope, what is? Answer: good-quality optics, a sturdy mount, and ease of use. There's a lot of choice in today's telescope marketplace, so here are a few things to keep in mind before you part with your hard-earned money.

Where to Buy   The best place to buy a quality telescope is from a store that specializes in selling astronomical equipment. There, the staff will be knowledgeable, not only about the instruments they sell but also about astronomy in general. To find these stores, check astronomy magazines for ads from scope manufacturers. Two of the major players, Celestron International *(www.celestron.com)* and Meade Instruments Corporation *(www.meade.com)*, list dealers who sell their products; those same retailers usually also carry scopes from other manufacturers as well as telescope accessories. A third major manufacturer, Orion Telescopes and Binoculars, is a web- and catalog-based retailer only *(www.telescope.com)*.

Some planetarium and science-center gift shops sell scopes, and if the sales clerk can't answer your questions, he or she will usually be able to find a staff member who can. Many camera stores also sell telescopes, although the staff at these shops may know very little about what they're selling. Avoid the big-box retail outlets; the scope quality is likely to be as low as the price.

Whether you're shopping online, via mail order, or in a store, you can't test a scope's performance until you actually buy it and try it out under the stars. So be sure to ask about the vendor's return policy and, if possible, get a copy of it in writing.

Aperture Size   As with binoculars, the bigger the telescope's aperture (the size of its main mirror or lens), the more you'll see: more faint objects and more detail in brighter objects. But scopes with big apertures are not only expensive, they're

WHAT DO YOU WANT TO OBSERVE?

Even the best scope won't be the best for all kinds of observing. And certain types of telescopes are better suited for some kinds of observing than others.

REFRACTORS in the 3- to 4-inch (75- to 100-mm) range are good for observing the Moon, planets, double stars, and brighter star clusters and nebulas, but their lack of light-gathering power (that small aperture) makes them less than ideal for viewing galaxies or anything faint. A good refractor will cost you more per inch of aperture than other types of scopes.

heavy. And you won't see anything at all if yours is stashed in a closet or hidden in a basement because it's too bulky and takes too much effort to drag outside and set up. An inexpensive, small-aperture telescope that can be ready to use in five minutes or loaded into the back of the car for a quick trip to a nearby park will probably give you a lot more bang for your buck. Get the largest aperture you can afford but that's small enough to be portable.

How small is too small? Avoid apertures of less than 3 inches

NEWTONIAN REFLECTORS with a low f/ratio (f/5 or less, such as the short-tube f/4 StarBlast on the left) are good for finding faint nebulas and galaxies, star clusters, and wide-field views of the Milky Way, and they're okay for the Moon and planets. Those with a high f/ratio (f/6 or larger, such as the long-tube f/8 SkyQuest at right) are best for high-magnification views of solar-system objects, double stars, and bright deep-sky objects. Newtonian Reflectors do have one advantage over refractors and "cats": they're the least-expensive scope per inch of aperture.

So, what should you buy if you're just starting out and don't know what you want to observe? A good telescope to start with is a 4- to 8-inch (100- to 200-mm) reflector with an f/ratio between f/5 and f/8. An all-purpose scope, it will give you decent views of just about everything. Sooner or later, though, you'll probably end up buying a second telescope to complement the first.

SMALL CATADIOPTRIC SCOPES, with apertures up to 5 inches (125 mm), are generally good for the Moon, planets, and double stars. But they usually have a very narrow field of view, so they're not great for observing wide-field star clusters or great swaths of the Milky Way. They're often sold with Go-To mounts, which can boost their price considerably. (The "cat" in the photo, above, is a Go To scope: for more on these, see page 129.)

(75 mm). While there are some very good (and very expensive) refractors of this size, you'll find yourself restricted to viewing the Moon, planets, and other objects big and bright enough to be seen with an aperture that small. An inexpensive 3-inch (75-mm) or larger scope, on the other hand, will show you faint nebulas and galaxies, in addition to the brighter sights.

F/ratio One number you'll often hear mentioned when star-gazers "talk telescopes" is the f/ratio of an instrument. So you might hear "My f/4 gives me great views of the Milky Way." You may also see this number on the telescope itself. What is it, and why is it important?

The *f/ratio*, also known as the *focal ratio*, is the scope's focal length divided by its aperture (in millimeters). To figure out the f/ratio, you first need to know the telescope's *focal length*. That's the distance, also in millimeters, from the scope's primary mirror (or lens) to the point where an image comes to a focus. In most telescopes (except catadioptrics), the focal length is about equal to the length of the tube. (Often the number is stamped right on the scope, or, if not, you'll find it in the instruction manual.) So, a scope with an 8-inch (200-mm) aperture and a focal length of 2,000 mm has a focal ratio of f/10.

The f/ratio becomes important when deciding what astronomical sights you really want to observe. Two telescopes with the same aperture but different f/ratio—say, f/4 and f/8—for example, will have different advantages: the short-tube f/4 scope will give you great, low-power, wide-field views of the Milky Way, nebulas, and star clusters, but the long-tube f/8 will let you boost the magnification, for excellent high-power views of the Moon, planets, and double stars.

Mounts and Tripods   A scope with great optics is useless without a sturdy mount and tripod. (Mounts and tripods generally come together as one unit.) There are two main types of mounts—*altazimuth* and *equatorial*—plus a variation on the altazimuth called a *Dobsonian*. (See the glossary on page 131.)

A Dobsonian is a reflector on an altazimuth mount that swivels on its base (azimuth) and rocks up and down (altitude) on the tube's pivot point. While it may sound complicated, tracking an object with a well-built Dobsonian requires only the lightest of touches.

An altazimuth mount is simple to use and is common on inexpensive refractors. The better versions come with manual slow-motion controls for both the up-down (altitude) and side-to-side (azimuth) motions, so you can easily fine-tune the scope's aim, although to track an object you have to move the scope in both directions simultaneously.

An equatorial mount is sturdier and more complicated to properly set up than an altazimuth, but with one axis aimed at Polaris, the Pole Star, it allows you to easily track objects in the sky by moving the scope in only a single direction. The mount should come with manual slow-motion controls, though many have a single-axis motor drive as a standard feature.

A Dobsonian is a version of an altazimuth mount used with reflectors. Aiming a "Dob" is a simple matter of pushing or pulling the tube until the object is found, something that's easily done, especially when the scope is small.

How do you tell if a scope has a decent mount? Gently tap the scope while looking at a distant object. If the view jumps around briefly and then settles down, your mount is okay. A view that wobbles around for several seconds means using the scope will be an exercise in frustration every time you touch the scope to re-aim it or improve the focus. If

An altazimuth mount supports this small refractor. The mount's manual slow-motion controls (on flexible cables) help you smoothly track celestial objects without having to touch the telescope.

the mount is poor, you'll find yourself spending more time waiting around for everything to settle down than actually observing. Small refractors are notorious for having "wobble mounts"; supplying a cheap mount and tripod is one way manufacturers keep the cost down.

Some telescope mounts include motors that let you aim the scope with the push of a couple of buttons on a small hand paddle. Some of these hand controllers are actually computers that will find and automatically track celestial objects, which means you don't have to manually adjust the scope's aim every few moments. Don't confuse motorized mounts with Go To scopes, however (see more on these, below).

Go To Telescopes   Locating faint targets in a light-polluted city sky can be a major challenge. You're likely to spend more time searching for an object than observing it. This is why a Go To telescope can be very appealing. A Go To scope comes equipped with a computer: when you enter an object's name into its hand controller, it will find and follow any celestial sight included in its database. Sounds easy—except that you still have to know a little about the sky to first set it up properly. A Go To won't go where you ask it to if it's not correctly initialized.

Go To Controllers

There's a computer in each of these Go To telescope hand controllers. Select an object from its database (or key in your favorite celestial sight), and the computer in the Meade or Celestron hand paddle will cause the telescope to "go to" that object. The Orion controller (right) works differently. It will tell you which way to push your scope's tube until the object you're looking for is centered in the eyepiece.

The downside? They're more expensive than a similar-sized scope that comes without the computer. In other words, you get less aperture for your money. For about the cost of a 4-inch (100-mm) Go To, it's possible to buy a noncomputerized instrument with a 6- or 8-inch (150- or 200-mm) aperture. A simpler version of a Go To is a *Push To*. These are Dobsonian mounts that come with a "smart" hand controller, rather than a motor. After a simple set-up, you enter the object you want to find and start aiming the scope. When the display on the hand paddle reaches zero, the object should be visible in the eyepiece. As you might expect, a scope with a Push To controller will cost more than one without (but less than a Go To mount).

Supporting this reflector is a German equatorial mount. With one axis aimed at Polaris, an equatorial mount lets you move the scope in a single east-west motion in order to track your celestial target.

Other Considerations How awkward is the scope to use? Move the scope around; aim it low and high. Can you easily peer through the eyepiece regardless of where the scope is pointed? On a reflector, can you rotate the telescope's tube, so you're not forced into an awkward position to look through the eyepiece? Crouching or kneeling for long periods of time can be uncomfortable; you shouldn't have to be a contortionist to use a telescope.

Eyepieces

Your telescope won't need *this* many eyepieces to function. But most observers do have a set of three or four eyepieces that provide different magnifications for different observing purposes: from low power for wide-field views to high power for planetary observing.

Will you be doing any astrophotography? These days, just about any telescope/digital-camera combination will let you take pictures of the Moon and Sun (using a proper filter, of course). The planets are a bit more challenging but still within the reach of simple scopes. To take great shots of galaxies and nebulas, however, you'll need a quality equatorial mount, a telescope that's a step above a starter scope, and a lot of patience, as you try to make all the technology work. (See more in Chapter Eleven: Astrophotography.)

How Much to Spend Expect to spend *at least* $200 to $300 for a decent starter telescope, plus possibly another $100 for some extras. There are very few good telescopes to be had for

Finders

A *finder* is a low-power, wide-field viewer attached to your big telescope to help you locate celestial sights. They come in two styles. One, called a *finderscope*, looks like a mini-telescope (right); make sure it has a magnification of at least 6x, or it will be frustrating to use. The other is a *reflex* or *unit-power* finder (left), which doesn't magnify the view but merely projects a red dot onto the sky.

less, and most of the cheaper scopes fail in either optical quality or in the sturdiness of their mounts and tripods. If you're able to spend up to $400 on a scope, your choice of quality instruments will greatly increase.

Accessories

Eyepieces   Every telescope comes with an eyepiece (some manufacturers provide two). But you'll want a variety of them—in a range of focal lengths—to use for different viewing purposes. Low-power eyepieces give you a wide field of view and are better when there's atmospheric turbulence. High-power eyepieces magnify the image more, giving you a close-up view with more detail. But generally speaking, you'll use low-power eyepieces much more often than high-power ones because the seeing often won't be steady enough to allow crisp, clear views at high magnifications.

Most moderately priced telescopes use standard eyepieces with barrels 1.25 inches (31.7 mm) in diameter; more expensive scopes accept 2-inch (50.8 mm) eyepieces. Avoid scopes that take only 0.965-inch eyepieces.

References   The star maps in this book will hold you in good stead for a while, but eventually, you'll want to buy a good star atlas to help you discover new deep-sky wonders. A subscription to one of the major astronomy magazines will keep you informed about what's happening in the sky each month and which seasonal objects might be visible in your new scope.

GLOSSARY OF TELESCOPE TERMS

Achromat: a refractor with an objective lens made from two pieces of glass. Achromats are inexpensive scopes compared to apochromats.

Altazimuth mount: a simple mount in which one axis moves left/right (azimuth) while the other moves up/down (altitude).

Aperture: the diameter, in inches or millimeters, of the telescope's main mirror or lens.

Apochromat: a refractor with an objective lens made from two or more pieces of specially coated, expensive glass. These scopes cost more than achromats but give better views of celestial objects.

Dobsonian mount: a version of the altazimuth mount that's designed especially for reflectors.

Equatorial mount: a mount that has one axis pointed toward the celestial pole so that the scope can move north/south and east/west.

Focal length: the distance (in millimeters) between a primary mirror or lens and the point where the image is in focus.

Focal ratio (or f/ratio): the telescope's focal length (in millimeters) divided by its aperture (also in millimeters); written as an f/number (as in f/5 or f/12). Don't mix inches and millimeters; to convert to millimeters, multiply inches by 25.4.

Go To: a telescope with motors attached to each axis and an onboard computer that will find and track celestial objects.

Magnification: how much any given eyepiece/telescope combination enlarges the view. It's calculated by dividing the telescope's focal length by the focal length of the eyepiece. (The number on the side or top of the eyepiece is its focal length [in mm]).

Objective: the primary lens or mirror of a telescope.

Power: a description of the magnification. 100X means 100 power or 100-times magnification.

Push To: a Dobsonian with an electronic tracker (but no motor) that will help you find celestial objects.

CHAPTER ELEVEN
ASTROPHOTOGRAPHY

Have you ever witnessed a lovely sunset scene with the crescent Moon and brilliant Venus hanging low in a twilight sky and thought, "Gee, that would make a great picture"? Or looked up at a sky full of stars and wondered whether your camera would pick up those myriad points of light? Capturing scenes like these is a lot easier than it used to be, though when it comes to astrophotography, in many cases you can't just "point and shoot." With a little advanced planning

and the right equipment, however, you can take sky shots similar to many of those used in this book.

In this chapter, you'll find out how to get started in astrophotography using a camera either mounted on a tripod or piggybacked on a telescope. Advanced sky shooting with a camera, CCD imager, or webcam attached directly to a telescope is beyond the scope of this book.

Star Trails Alan Dyer took this four-hour exposure of star trails over Las Campanas Observatory in Chile.

THE CAMERA

Chances are, you already own a camera; will it work for astrophotography? Probably—unless it's a "point and shoot" model. While both digital and film cameras can be used for sky shooting, if yours is a point-and-shoot model, its use will be limited. It likely has a "sunset" or "night" setting that may give you decent twilight scenes but little else. A key requirement for astrophotography is a camera that allows you to override any automatic settings and keep the shutter open for up to a minute, preferably longer. If your camera can do this, you're on your way.

Believe it or not, this vintage Kodak Junior SIX-20 is capable of taking time-exposure photos of the night sky.

Film vs. Digital

The best *film* camera to use is an SLR (single-lens reflex). It lets you view the scene you're about to shoot through the same lens that takes the picture and gives you the option of using different lenses. In fact, many experienced astrophotographers prefer the old-fashioned, battery-free, manual SLRs that lack automatic settings. If you've got one tucked away in a closet, dig it out. As long as it has a B (bulb) setting that lets you take a time-exposure shot, you're in business. If you don't have one and you'd like to, check out used-camera shops for a reconditioned model.

Modern SLRs with lots of automatic features will work, too. Many have preprogrammed settings that will let you take time exposures; others actually have a B setting, although an electronic cable release may be needed to activate it. The drawback is that multiple exposures of longer than a minute will tend to rapidly drain the camera's batteries.

The great thing about going *digital* is that the photo you just took can be immediately displayed on the camera's built-in LCD screen. This is a big help when you're shooting the sky. Since exposure times are often little more than educated guesses, being able to take a picture and immediately see if it's under or overexposed lets you quickly zero in on the proper setting. And because the camera stores the images on a reusable memory card, you can keep on shooting, discarding the failed shots, until you achieve the result you want.

Most midlevel consumer digital cameras will work for astrophotography, assuming they have manual overrides for focus and aperture, variable ISO levels up to at least 800, and settings that let you take thirty- or sixty-second exposures. The images may look "noisy" (the digital equivalent of film grain), however. If a digital camera is in your future, and you want to use it for astrophotography, look for a model that has noise-reduction circuitry, a feature that helps suppress the electronic noise that builds up during time exposures. The ultimate electronic camera is a digital SLR; some models can capture night-sky scenes that are as good as anything shot using film.

THE FILM

Prints or slides? That's the dilemma facing anyone using film to shoot the sky. Prints are handy for showing off your work, but to get them, you have to either have the prints generated by a machine that knows nothing about the oddities of astrophotography or take your film to a custom lab where they'll ultimately do it right—but charge you a lot of money. Using slide film avoids the printing-process problems and, generally, gives good results, but showing off your handiwork can be a bit awkward. Most veteran astrophotographers suggest that beginners start with slide film. Of course, both slides and prints can also be turned into digital images.

Fast or faster? The sky is dark, and the stars are dim, so fast films (those with high ISO numbers) that will quickly capture as much light as possible are best, right? Not necessarily. Slow-speed film records sharper detail than high-speed film and doesn't suffer from excessive grain. For the type of astrophotography we're discussing in this chapter, films with an ISO of 200, 400, or 800 will be fine.

What film? It seems that every couple of years, film manufacturers either "improve" an old film or come out with a new one and discontinue an old favorite. Even worse, some manufacturers are getting out of the film business altogether. So recommending a suitable film isn't a simple matter. If these slide films are available, try Kodak Ektachrome E200 (EPD Professional or the consumer version) or Fujichrome Provia 100F or 400F. A good print film is Kodak Royal Gold 200. Regardless of which one you choose, your best bet is to experiment: buy a roll, shoot, and see how it turns out. Don't forget to make notes as you take each photo, so you can compare what you did with the results you get. Eventually, you'll settle on a personal favorite.

GETTING STARTED

This chapter will get you started in astrophotography using three basic techniques: by mounting your camera on a tripod, mounting it on a telescope, and holding it to a telescope's eyepiece. Whichever way you try, it's important to experiment: treat the information in each project as only a starting point. And don't be discouraged if your first efforts don't look like the images in this chapter. The photographer who took most of them started out with a simple camera mounted on a tripod and is still experimenting (and making mistakes) after more than thirty years of sky shooting.

TIPS AND TRICKS

• Read the camera manual before stepping outside to shoot, especially if your camera has various automatic functions that you'll have to override and/or manually change.

• If your camera has an autofocus mode, turn it off. Manually set the focus to infinity (the ∞ symbol). If the focusing ring on the lens is loose, consider taping it so the focus doesn't stray.

• For astrophotography, the faster the lens (in other words, the smaller the aperture number) the better—up to a point. An ideal aperture setting is f/2.8; anything faster (f/2 or f/1.4) may give you distorted star images beyond the center of the image frame, due to lens flaws. If your lens won't open to f/2.8, set it as wide as possible (as small an aperture number as possible).

• If you're using an SLR camera, a wide-angle (20- to 35-mm) or normal (50-mm) lens will be best for the techniques described here. A short (up to 200-mm) telephoto lens may come in handy, but avoid using a zoom lens (except for twilight scenes), unless that's all you have, because these lenses are usually pretty slow.

Setting Up the Camera

To shoot the sky, you can use your camera in a number of ways: through the eyepiece of your telescope, riding piggyback on your scope, or by mounting it on a tripod. All of the images in this chapter were shot using one of these three methods.

Through the Eyepiece

The simplest way to use your telescope for astrophotography is to hold a camera up to the eyepiece and snap a photo of a bright object, such as the Moon. You can handhold the camera, mount it on a separate tripod (both are awkward options), or buy a bracket like the one shown here that lets you attach the camera directly to the eyepiece.

Piggyback Sky Shooting

If you have a telescope with an equatorial mount and a motor drive, attaching your camera to your scope will let you track the stars as you take a picture. Many scopes have a mounting bracket, so the camera can be attached directly to it, but a more flexible solution is to put a ball-and-socket tripod head on that bracket, and then attach your camera to the ball joint.

Camera-on-Tripod Sky Shooting

The simplest way to start photographing the sky is to attach a camera to a tripod. A sturdy tripod is critical; make sure its head can be solidly locked in place and that its leg extensions won't slip. A cable release to activate the shutter (and keep it open) is essential. Old-fashioned manual SLRs use a mechanical release; digital and auto-everything film cameras need an electronic remote control.

PROJECTS TO SHOOT

You don't need an expensive camera and telescope to capture beautiful scenes of the night sky. An old camera and a tripod are all you need to take a variety of celestial portraits.

Project 1: Shooting Twilight Scenes

A good time to start if you've never tried taking photos of the sky is at dusk (or at dawn if you're an early riser). Forego the usual generic sunset/sunrise scenics, though, and check to see if the crescent Moon and/or some bright planets are arrayed in the twilight sky. If so, go out, and start shooting. Try different lenses—wide angle, normal, telephoto, even a zoom lens—but make sure the aperture is set to f/2.8 and that the lens really is focused at infinity. Also try to vary your exposure times (called bracketing). Start by noting what your camera thinks the exposure should be, then switch to manual mode and shoot a series of images at shutter speeds faster and slower than the "predicted" exposure. Make notes of what you're doing (especially if you're using film), so that you can determine which combination of lens and exposure time gives the most pleasing result.

If your camera has no manual override but does have an automatic mode or sunset setting, try it anyway, particularly in the early evening. You may be surprised at the results.

Venus and Saturn with the Moon

Twilight (and even post-twilight) sky scenes benefit from the presence of an interesting foreground. Here, the crescent Moon, with brilliant Venus above it and faint Saturn directly below, hangs over a city skyline. The shot was taken using a camera on a tripod, an 80-mm lens, ISO 100 slide film, and a four-second exposure at f/2.8.

Big Dipper and Old Faithful

This wide-angle view of the Big Dipper is striking because it includes a landscape: Old Faithful geyser in Yellowstone National Park, Wyoming. To capture a scene like this, timing is as important as the camera settings: ISO 400, 28-mm lens at f/2.8, and a thirty-second exposure. Light from the full Moon illuminates the foreground.

Project 2: Shooting Star Scenes

Once you've tried some scenic twilight shots, photographing stars and constellations can be your next step. With nothing more than a camera and tripod, you can easily record stars and constellations, even from a light-polluted city. Use ISO 400 or 800 (film or digital-camera settings), and a 28- or 50-mm lens. A 50-mm lens takes in a wide enough swath of the sky (about 40° by 27°) to capture most constellations; for larger constellations, use a 28-mm lens (it gives a 65° by 46° field of view).

The key is to experiment with different exposures and ISO settings (or different film speeds). A sixty-second exposure on ISO 400 film will capture the same amount of starlight as a thirty-second exposure on ISO 800 film. The faster ISO lets you use shorter shutter speeds, but the image may look grainier. But the slower ISO (and therefore the longer exposure) could result in the stars appearing as streaks. While you can get very creative with star-trail astrophotography (see opening image), there are times when you want the stars to look like points of light. How long you can keep the shutter open without the stars trailing depends on which lens you use and what part of the sky you're shooting. The table below will help you determine the maximum exposure possible to get non-trailed star scenes.

Lens	Near the celestial equator	Near the celestial pole
28 mm	30 seconds	90 seconds
50 mm	15 seconds	45 seconds
100 mm	7 seconds	22 seconds
200 mm	3 seconds	11 seconds

While stars are nice, consider creating a "nightscape" that includes some landscape.

Project 3: Make a Constellation Album

Once you've determined what combination of ISO setting (or film), exposure time, and camera lens gives you the most pleasing star-field results, consider starting a constellation album. Avoid shooting when the Moon is present; for this project, its light isn't welcome. This is a year-long project!

An interesting side project is to shoot one set of constellations from the city and another from a dark-sky site, using the same lens, ISO, and exposure setting. The result is a powerful visual demonstration to your friends of the effects of light pollution on the night sky.

And if you're traveling south of the equator, take your astrophotography gear along, so you can shoot some of the Southern Hemisphere constellations that you never see from your backyard.

Star Trails over the Badlands

When shooting star-trails, the presence of moonlight isn't necessarily bad. It can illuminate the foreground, giving a real sense of depth to the scene. In this thirty-minute exposure (with ISO 50 film and an 80-mm lens), the rising full Moon illuminates a hoodoos formation in Dinosaur Provincial Park in Alberta, Canada.

Project 4: Shooting Star Trails

It seems easy and obvious. To create star-trail images, attach your camera to a tripod, open the shutter, and forget about it for an hour or two. What could be simpler? Well, there actually is more to it than that. First, you need a really dark, light-pollution-free sky, especially if you're doing exposures of more than an hour. Excess light will show up on long exposures as an unwanted glow and wash out the stars. (Plus, long exposures leave your lens vulnerable to dew.) High-speed film isn't necessary; an ISO level as low as 50 or 100 can produce excellent results. (However, you may have to experiment with different films, because many film emulsions turn green during long exposures.) Don't set the aperture wide open; close it to f/4 or f/5.6. Try a sequence of different exposures; start with fifteen minutes and work your way up. And consider where in the sky you're pointing your camera. If you aim toward Polaris, your star trails will be circular; point it toward the celestial equator and the trails will be nearly straight.

Because of the long exposures, star-trail photography takes time. In any given evening, you might end up with only five or six shots. Double your output by borrowing a camera and tripod (don't forget the cable release). That way, you can have two cameras going at once.

Big Dipper and Arcturus

This wide-angle view of the Big Dipper (and most of Ursa Major) and Arcturus was captured on ISO 400 slide film using a 28-mm lens at f/3.5.

Auroral Meteor

Sometimes you get lucky. The photographer was shooting a brilliant aurora over Steamboat Springs, Colorado, when a Perseid meteor fell through the multicolored sky. The twenty-second exposure was shot using a 50-mm lens at f1.8 on Kodak Max 400 film; the camera was tripod mounted.

Project 5: Shooting Meteors

Capturing a meteor is generally a case of dumb luck. The process is a combination of constellation and star-trail photography: use ISO 400 or 800 film and a regular or wide-angle lens; set your camera on a tripod and aim it at an area of the sky; open the shutter; and wait (with your fingers crossed). If you see a meteor and you think it passed through your camera's field of view, close the shutter right away and start another exposure. If you don't see a meteor after five or ten minutes, close the shutter and start another exposure. This brief exposure will keep the star trails short (making a meteor more obvious) and prevent light pollution from washing out the sky and your image. While random meteors can be seen every evening, you'll want to try shooting during a meteor shower (see Chapter Seven for dates).

But what if you have a digital camera? If you can adjust it so it will automatically take a never-ending sequence of thirty-second exposures one right after the other, then you can let the camera continuously photograph a section of the sky and hope it captures a meteor! (Make sure the lens is wide open and focused on infinity, and set the ISO rating to 800.)

Space Station Trail

Even from the city, the International Space Station is easy to spot—and photograph. To the eye it looks like a slowly moving dot, but a camera accumulates its light over time and shows it as a streak. This thirty-second exposure on ISO 100 film with a 28-mm lens shows the Space Station passing between clouds and two bright stars: Deneb (left of the ISS) and Vega (right).

Project 6: Shooting Satellites

Capturing a bright satellite like the International Space Station (ISS) is easy; all it takes is a little advanced planning. Use a website such as *www.heavens-above.com* to determine when the ISS will be visible from your area, how bright it will get (it can reach magnitude −5), and what part of the sky it will pass through. Set up your camera and tripod as if you were doing constellation photography. When you spot the ISS, it will look like a slowly moving dot of light. As it enters your camera's field of view, open the shutter. The length of the exposure will determine the length of the streak you'll see in your image. But be warned: on each pass, the station will be visible for a maximum of only a few minutes.

Also visible are flares from Iridium satellites, caused by sunlight glinting off their antenna arrays. The glint is short-lived; only a few seconds in duration. So the real challenge to photographing an Iridium flare is making sure your camera is pointed in the right direction (websites like Heaven's Above will help). An exposure of thirty seconds, centered on the time of the flare, will capture the event.

Project 7: Shooting the Aurora

A camera-tripod combination is the best way to capture a display of the aurora borealis (northern lights). Use 200 or 400 ISO film or digital settings, and a 28-mm lens. Vary your exposure times depending on the brightness of the northern lights: thirty to forty-five seconds for a faint display, as little as five or ten seconds for a bright one. The aurora can ripple and change color with amazing speed; shorter exposures will help freeze the celestial action.

Unfortunately, the precise time and date when a display of the northern lights may appear cannot be predicted, though there are several websites that try to do just that (see the Resources section). AstroAlerts from *Sky & Telescope* *http://SkyandTelescope.com/observing/proamcollab/astroalert/article_332_1.asp* are email warnings, or, for a fee, Spaceweather Phone *(www.spaceweatherphone.com/)* will call you when a display might be imminent.

Dancing Lights

The camera often records what the eye can't see. Not only will a time-exposure photo reveal stars too dim to see with the naked eye, it will also pick up unexpected color. Many displays of the northern lights look green to the eye, but a camera often records rays of red or purple. This scene of an aurora over a town and nearby lake was captured using a 28-mm lens and a thirty-second exposure on ISO 400 film.

Project 8: Shooting Lunar Eclipses

Photographing totality during a lunar eclipse is challenging because you never know how dark the Moon might get. And if you want the eclipsed Moon to be anything other than a tiny dot in the image, you'll need at least a 300-mm telephoto lens. Fortunately, totality is a leisurely affair that can last an hour or more, giving you plenty of time to experiment with your camera settings. Here's where a digital camera with a telephoto lens really shines. Be sure to manually set the focus to infinity, the ISO to 800, and the aperture to f/2.8, then start shooting using an exposure range from ¼-second down to four seconds. Look at your results. If the Moon is too dark, boost the ISO and try again. With a 300-mm lens, don't expose for more than two seconds, or the Moon will blur due to the motion of the sky.

With a film camera you have to commit to a film speed before the event starts, so all you can do is bracket and hope for the best. Or you can create an eclipse trail. Use ISO 100 or 200 film, attach a 28-mm (wide-angle) lens, set the aperture to

f/11 or f/16, and you're ready. When the eclipse is scheduled to start, position the Moon in one corner of the camera's viewfinder and align the camera so the Moon will drift diagonally across the field of view. (Use a planetarium program or an online star chart to figure out the Moon's motion during the eclipse.) Lock the shutter open with the cable release, watch the eclipse, and at the end, release the shutter.

A Lunar Eclipse from Beginning to End

With proper planning, a single frame can capture an entire lunar eclipse. A camera (with ISO 100 film) on a tripod and a 28-mm lens set to f/16 recorded the partial phases. To capture the totally eclipsed Moon, the lens was covered for about a minute at mid-totality. The aperture was then opened f/2.8 and the lens uncovered for sixty seconds. It was covered again for another minute, the aperture reset to f/16, and the exposure continued for the duration of the eclipse.

Project 9: Shooting Solar Eclipses

Shooting totality during a solar eclipse is an exercise in panic control: the sight of the blackened Sun surrounded by its corona can cause you to forget all your carefully laid photography plans. Totality is short, and if you've never experienced it before, think carefully about whether you really want to spend most of those precious few moments looking at the eclipse through a camera's viewfinder.

If you'd like to have a photographic memento, consider these hints. A 200-mm lens is about the minimum needed for a small, but pleasing, image size. Slow film or a low ISO setting (50 to 200) is best. Manually set the focus to infinity and the aperture to f/4 or f/5.6. If you can set your camera to automatically trigger the shutter every one or two seconds, then use this function to record the diamond ring. Stop it once the Sun is completely eclipsed. The quickest way to get a record of totality is to bracket. Shoot an image sequence in which the exposure changes from $\frac{1}{500}$-second down to four seconds (without changing the aperture setting). Now stop. Look up. Don't miss the visual beauty of a total solar eclipse.

Totality
A total eclipse of the Sun is a stunning spectacle that lasts mere moments, so careful planning is required. This shot of totality was taken with a 200-mm lens at f/4 on ISO 100 film; the white dot at lower left is Jupiter.

Winter Milky Way (Auriga, Gemini, and Taurus)
This fifteen-minute exposure (ISO 200 film, 28-mm lens at f/2.8) shows part of the winter Milky Way and includes the constellations Taurus (at right; note the Pleiades), Auriga, and Gemini. Capturing a scene like this isn't possible unless you can track the sky with your camera.

Project 10: Piggyback Astrophotography

If you've exhausted the various camera-on-tripod possibilities, consider turning your telescope into a mount for your camera. This is the basis of piggyback astrophotography, so-called because the camera rides piggyback-style on the telescope.

This type of sky shooting requires a telescope with a motor drive and an equatorial mount. (A Go To scope on an altazimuth mount won't work because of how the computer incrementally moves the telescope on two axes to track the sky.) It also involves making sure the telescope is carefully aligned with Polaris; otherwise the photographic result will include trailed stars. Finally, you need a dark sky. Piggyback photography in a city will yield mostly disappointing results.

Although the camera gear needed is no different from basic tripod astrophotography, you may discover that your favorite film doesn't perform well. Most film doesn't like being exposed to light (even if it's just starlight) for more than a minute or two, and the film emulsion will sometimes turn green during a long exposure. Once again, experimentation is the key. Try different exposure/film combinations (don't expose for longer than fifteen minutes, to start with, until you can see some results), don't be afraid to use telephoto lenses, and whatever you do, keep careful notes.

Project 11: Shooting the Moon

If you own a telescope, you may have wondered how easy (or hard) it is to take a picture through it. For a bright object like the Moon, it's remarkably easy—if you have a digital camera. Simply aim your scope at the Moon, put in your lowest-power eyepiece, and focus it. Then hold the lens of your camera as close to the eyepiece as possible, and shoot! This is called *afocal* photography, and it's the way amateurs took photos through their telescopes in the days before SLRs with their removable lenses became readily available.

There are some pitfalls and problems, however. First, you'll probably see a tunnel of darkness surrounding the image. Use the camera's optical (not digital) zoom to enlarge the image and avoid this vignetting. You'll also find it hard to hold the digital camera steady and keep the Moon, scope, and camera in perfect alignment. So, if this type of sky shooting appeals to you, you'll soon be looking for either a bracket clamp to hold the camera above the eyepiece (see the photo on page 135) or an adaptor ring that directly attaches the camera lens to the eyepiece. (For more information, see the astrophotography section in the Resources section, page 150.)

Lunar Close Up

It's possible to hold a camera to the eyepiece of a telescope pointed at the Moon, snap a picture, and get a decent image! A digital camera is the best way to go; because you can see the results immediately, you can keep trying until you get the best possible image.

CHAPTER TWELVE
ASTRO-TRAVEL

ooner or later—and if you get hooked on stargazing, it
will be sooner—you're going to want to venture
beyond the confines of your backyard and local observing sites and explore what the rest of the world's skies have to
offer. After all, if an eclipse won't come to you (remember, the
odds are one in 375), then you're going to have to go to it.

Fortunately, that isn't hard to do. Astro-travel has become popular in recent years, and tour companies either offering or specializing in astro-travel abound. How do you find them? A good place to start is in the various astronomy magazines. Tour companies will usually advertise in their pages—especially in the months leading up to a major event such as an eclipse or transit. In fact, it's not unusual for eclipse tours to be advertised as early as two years in advance. Some, to the more exotic locales (Turkey, Greece) fill up quickly, so even though two years may sound like a lot of lead time, you don't want to wait too long to book your trip.

Eclipse Trips

You don't have to book a vacation with an astro-travel company, but eclipses are often only visible from pretty out-of-the way places. If you're an experienced traveler (and the *Rough Guide* is your travel bible), with some advance planning there's no reason not to organize your own trip. Keep in mind, though, that tour companies will have booked anything worth sleeping in for miles around the viewing path, so it may be a safer bet to sign up with one of them.

Of course, sometimes the path of totality runs through some really obscure locales, and then it's definitely best to seek out a tour company. A recent solar eclipse visible from Antarctica, for example, would have been impossible to experience without booking with a tour group. Two companies even offered views of that eclipse from aboard a plane!

Probably the best way to see a total eclipse of the Sun is on an eclipse cruise. Wildly popular, eclipse cruises offer a number of advantages, not the least of which is the ship's maneuverability. If the clouds start rolling in, a ship has the advantage of being

The great thing about seeing an eclipse in an exotic locale (such as Turkey, above) is that there's still something to see when the eclipse is over (or if it's clouded out).

able to steam toward a distant patch of clear sky (there's usually a meteorologist on board to point the ship in the right direction), while those viewing from shore are restricted to the available roads, most of which are either jammed with like-minded observers or running in the wrong direction.

Clear skies are never guaranteed, of course; getting clouded out is one of the risks you face with any celestial event (there's no rain date), so be prepared for possible disappointment. Plan to enjoy the experience, regardless of what happens, and take a few days before or after the eclipse to do some sightseeing. Don't make your trip just about the eclipse.

Eclipse cruises are wildly popular with observers of all ages.

Catching Some Rays

Somewhat less exotic, but still popular, are aurora tours. Requisite gear in your luggage, though, will be down parkas and thick, woolly mittens; if you sign up for an aurora tour, you'll be heading for places like Alaska, Iceland, northern Canada, and Scandinavia. As with eclipses, those glorious dancing lights can be obscured by cloud at times (or be faint and unspectacular), so be sure to book a trip that offers other diversions.

Popular as they are, eclipse trips and aurora tours aren't the only offerings on the astro-travel menu. Many companies offer a variety of trips, ranging from observatory tours to general stargazing in dark-sky locales. These are often paired with daytime excursions, such as whale-watching or studying cave paintings.

Big scopes, small cost. Star parties can attract thousands of observers, many of whom bring along an arsenal of optical equipment. Best of all, they don't mind sharing the view.

Astronomy B&Bs

If you're not into arranged tours and want an astrofriendly, self-styled vacation, consider booking yourself into an astronomy B&B. Accommodations with a view, they often come complete with dark skies, an onsite astronomer, and a well-equipped observing site (sometimes, even a mini-observatory). You're welcome to bring your own scope or to share views with other guests through the B&B scopes. Sky tours are often available from the host, for an extra fee. As you might guess, astronomy B&Bs are usually located in dark-sky locations; many are in North America, but you'll find a number of them in other countries, as well.

The Large and Small Clouds of Magellan can be seen only in southern skies. Both are bright enough to be seen with the naked eye.

Heading South

For a real change of scenery, consider heading south of the equator, to Peru, perhaps, or Australia, and take a look at the sky from a completely different perspective. Not only will you see constellations and celestial objects you've never seen before, but it can be interesting to see familiar constellations (like Orion, for example) turned upside down. Just be sure to bring along a sky atlas that includes star charts for the Southern Hemisphere.

The beautiful Eta Carina Nebula is best viewed from the Southern Hemisphere.

Star Parties

Not exotic at all, star parties are nevertheless great opportunities to meet other recreational astronomers and spend some quality time under the stars. They also offer the opportunity to see the sky through a variety of telescopes, a real boon if your arsenal of optics only includes a small one—or none at all. Star parties can last anywhere from a few days to more than a week, often at campsites (some pretty rugged) in dark-sky areas. You can find more information about star parties through the astronomy clubs, or check the Resources section for web addresses for the larger parties.

RESOURCES

Getting Connected

There's a wealth of information out there for anyone looking for it, and, as a beginning stargazer, you probably are. Websites abound; a few clicks will get you started down any astronomical path you care to explore. A good place to start is with a couple of the major astronomy magazine websites, which offer all sorts of goodies: telescope and book reviews, sky charts, news articles, web links, image galleries, and a whole lot more.

You might also want to pick up their respective printed publications. The two largest are *Astronomy* and *Sky & Telescope*, which are widely available, even outside of North America. Or, check out *Night Sky*, Sky Publishing's magazine for novice skywatchers. Read through as many magazines as you can get your hands on and see which one appeals to you. Whichever one you choose will provide you with up-to-date news and information on astronomical events and happenings in the night sky.

Become familiar with your local planetarium and attend the star shows. They're a great way to learn more about the night sky (and you never have to worry about mosquitoes, frostbite, atmospheric turbulence, or clouds; under the planetarium dome, the skies are always clear and dark). Observatories can be fascinating places to visit; some offer regular tours. Check their websites for times.

Want company on your observing sessions? Join an astronomy club. There are hundreds of local chapters in North America and plenty more in countries around the world. You'll find websites listing clubs on page 154.

Lastly, you might want to consider investing in planetarium software. It can be a little tricky to set up (read some reviews first, to find the program that's best for you), but once you've got the hang of it, you'll appreciate the convenience of having daily sky charts that show you what the sky will look like from your own back yard. Use them to plan your next observing session, then get out under the stars!

Astronomy Websites by Subject

The information listed here is accurate as of late 2004; websites come and go, however, so you may find that some no longer exist or have changed URLs.

Links to Astronomical Sites
www.SkyandTelescope.com/resources/internet/
www.cv.nrao.edu/fits/www/astronomy.html
www.backyardastronomy.com/

The Sky Tonight
www.earthsky.org/skywatching/tsky.php
www.SkyandTelescope.com/observing/ataglance/
www.bbc.co.uk/science/space/myspace/nightsky/
http://observingthesky.org/

Clear Sky Clock (weather)
Covers locations in Canada, USA, and Mexico
www.cleardarksky.com/csk/

Sun and Moon Rise/Set Times (and more)
http://aa.usno.navy.mil/

Explore the Moon
www.lpod.org/

The Solar System
www.nineplanets.org/
www.lpl.arizona.edu/alpo/
http://photojournal.jpl.nasa.gov/index.html

Planetary Exploration
www.jpl.nasa.gov/
www.esa.int

The Sun
http://sohowww.nascom.nasa.gov/
www.SkyandTelescope.com/observing/objects/sun/
www.cv.nrao.edu/fits/www/yp_solar.html

Solar and Lunar Eclipses
http://sunearth.gsfc.nasa.gov/eclipse/eclipse.html
www.mreclipse.com/
www.SkyandTelescope.com/observing/objects/eclipses/

Lunar Occultations
www.SkyandTelescope.com/observing/objects/occultations/

Aurora predictions and information
www.sel.noaa.gov/
www.spacew.com/
www.geo.mtu.edu/weather/aurora/
www.SkyandTelescope.com/observing/proamcollab/astroalert/
www.spaceweatherphone.com/

Comets, Asteroids, and Meteors
www.comets.amsmeteors.org/
http://impact.arc.nasa.gov/index.html
http://cfa-www.harvard.edu/icq/icq.html
http://neo.jpl.nasa.gov/neo/

Satellite Observing
www.heavens-above.com/
www.satobs.org/satintro.html

Constellations
www.seds.org/Maps/Const/constS.html
www.dibonsmith.com/

The Messier & NGC Lists
www.seds.org/messier/
www.seds.org/~spider/ngc/ngc.html
www.starastronomy.org/Observing/Fell/

Online Star Charts
www.SkyandTelescope.com/observing/skychart/
www.skyviewcafe.com/skyview.php
www.astro.psu.edu/users/stark/viewing/
http://astro4.ast.vill.edu/skyglobe.htm

Discover the Stars
www.astro.uiuc.edu/~kaler/sow/

Scale of the Universe
http://heasarc.gsfc.nasa.gov/docs/cosmic/
www.wordwizz.com/pwrsof10.htm

Astronomy Picture of the Day (APOD)
http://antwrp.gsfc.nasa.gov/apod/

Ask the Astronomer
www.astronomycafe.net/

Debunking Astronomical Myths
www.badastronomy.com/

Research Observatory Photo Galleries
Anglo-Australian Observatory
www.aao.gov.au/images.html/

ESO
www.eso.org/outreach/gallery/astro/

Gemini
www.gemini.edu/index.php?option=com_gallery

Hubble Space Telescope
http://hubblesite.org/

NOAO
www.noao.edu/image_gallery/

Canada-France-Hawaii Telescope
www.cfht.hawaii.edu/HawaiianStarlight/

Dark Skies
International Dark Sky Association
www.darksky.org/

How dark is your observing site?
http://nineplanets.org/lm/rjm.html

Dark-Sky Sites: Is there a dark sky near you?
www.philharrington.net/dssd.htm

Planetarium Software
Lists of freeware and software
http://nineplanets.org/astrosoftware.html
www.SkyandTelescope.com/resources/software/

Desktop Universe
www.main-sequence.com/

Mac Astronomica
www.artistictechworks.com/astronomica.html

RedShift
www.redshift.de/

Astronomy Websites by Subject (continued)

SkyChart
www.southernstars.com/

SkyMap
www.skymap.com/

Starry Night
www.starrynight.com/

The Sky
www.bisque.com/

Astrophotography
Images are often for sale by the astrophotographer;
all are copyrighted.

Jeff Ball
www.earthandskyphoto.com/

Matt BenDaniel
www.starmatt.com/

António Cidadão
www.astrosurf.com/cidadao/

Chris Cook
www.abmedia.com/astro/

Bill and Sally Fletcher
www.scienceandart.com/

Robert Gendler
www.robgendlerastropics.com/

Ed Grafton
www.ghg.net/egrafton/

Tony and Daphne Hallas
www.astrophoto.com/

Phil Hoffman
www.picturetrail.com/gallery/view?p=6&uid=114235&

Thierry Legault
http://perso.club-internet.fr/legault/

Jerry Lodriguss
www.astropix.com/

Dennis Mammana
www.skyscapes.com/

Jack Newton
www.jacknewton.com/image_gallery.htm

Pekka Parviainen
www.polarimage.fi/

Damian Peach
www.damianpeach.com/

Philip Perkins
www.astrocruise.com/

Jerry Schad
www.skyphoto.com/

Loke Kun Tan
www.starryscapes.com/

How-to Articles on Astrophotography
www.astropix.com/HTML/I_ASTROP/TOC_AP.HTM
http://home.hiwaay.net/~krcool/Astro/asthwto/TriAst.htm
http://members.aol.com/tdcarls/simpleastrophotography.html
http://leonids.hq.nasa.gov/leonids/photo.html
http://SkyandTelescope.com/howto/imaging/
http://velatron.com/dca/

Major Telescope Manufacturers
Some will sell direct, others will list their retailers, most also
sell accessories.

Apogee
Variety of small refractors and Maksutovs
www.apogeeinc.com/

Astro-Physics
Premium refractors and Maksutovs
www.astro-physics.com/

Celestron International
Schmidt-Cassegrains, many small scopes
www.celestron.com/

Coronado Technology Group
Solar telescopes
www.coronadofilters.com/

Discovery Telescopes
Small Dobsonians
www.discovery-telescopes.com/

Meade Instruments
Schmidt-Cassegrains and other scopes
www.meade.com/

Orion Telescopes & Binoculars
Entry-level scopes of all types, as well as binoculars
www.telescope.com/

Pacific Telescope Corporation (Canada only)
Small scopes
www.skywatchertelescope.net/

Questar
Premium Maksutov-Cassegrains
www.questar-corp.com/

Stellarvue
Premium small refractors
www.stellarvue.com/

Takahashi
Very high-end refractors
www.takahashiamerica.com/

Tele Vue Optics
High-quality small refractors
www.televue.com/

Vixen North America
Premium small refractors
www.vixenamerica.com/

Major Binocular Manufacturers
Bushnell
www.bushnell.com/

Canon, Inc.
www.canon.com/

Celestron International
www.celestron.com/

Fujinon Inc.
www.fujinon.com/

Leica
www.leica-camera.com/

Nikon
www.nikonusa.com/

Olympus
www.olympusamerica.com/

Orion Telescopes & Binoculars
www.telescope.com/

Pentax
www.pentax.com/

Swift Instruments, Inc.
www.swift-optics.com/

Carl Zeiss, Inc.
www.zeiss.com/

Major Online Telescope and Accessory Retailers
Anacortes Telescope & Wild Bird
www.buytelescopes.com/

David Hinds Ltd. (United Kingdom)
www.dhinds.co.uk/

Hardin Optical Co.
www.hardin-optical.com/

Khan Scope Centre (Canada)
www.khanscope.com/

Oceanside Photo & Telescope
www.optcorp.com/

Orion Optics (United Kingdom)
www.orionoptics.co.uk/

Astronomy Websites by Subject *(continued)*

Telescope House (United Kingdom)
www.telescopehouse.co.uk/

Telescopes.com
www.telescopes.com/

List of Astronomical-Product Dealers
www.homestead.com/AstroWorld/dealers1.html
http://astronomy-mall.com/

List of Solar Filter Retailers
www.SkyandTelescope.com/observing/objects/sun/
 article_101_1.asp

Examples of Home-Built Observatories
http://nineplanets.org/obs/obslist.html
SkyandTelescope.com/howto/scopes/article_506_1.asp

Telescope Review Sites
Cloudy Nights Telescope Reviews
Quality of reviews ranges from skilled to amateurish
www.cloudynights.com/

Ed Ting's Telescope Review Web Site
Comprehensive site by knowledgeable reviewer
www.scopereviews.com/

Sky & Telescope Test Reports:
Pay site; reviews from the magazine in PDF format
www.SkyandTelescope.com/resources/testreports/

Astronomy Club Listings
World Wide listings (including USA):
www.SkyandTelescope.com/resources/organizations/
www.lpl.arizona.edu/~rhill/alpo/clublinks.html
www.astronomyclubs.com/

Night Sky Network (USA only)
nightsky.jpl.nasa.gov/

UK Astronomy
www.bbc.co.uk/science/space/myspace/localspace/index.shtml

Some Major Star Parties
www.texasstarparty.org (Texas)
www.stellafane.com (Vermont)
www.rtmc-inc.org (California)
www.scas.org/ (Florida)
www.oregonstarparty.org/ (Oregon)
nyaa-starfest.com/ (Ontario, Canada)

Planetarium Listings
www.lochness.com/lpco/lpco.html
www.ips-planetarium.org/atw/ips-around.html
www.SkyandTelescope.com/resources/organizations/

Astronomy News and Observing
Astronomical Society of the Pacific
www.astrosociety.org/

Astronomy **magazine**
http://astronomy.com

Astronomy & Space **magazine**
www.astronomy.ie/

Astronomy Now **magazine**
www.astronomynow.com/

Night Sky **magazine**
http://nightskymag.com/

SkyNews **magazine**
www.skynewsmagazine.com/

Sky & Telescope **magazine**
www.SkyandTelescope.com/

Space.com
www.space.com/

SpaceWeather.com
www.spaceweather.com/

StarDate **magazine**
www.stardate.org/

Universe Today
www.universetoday.com/

Suggested Books

Night-Sky Observing
- *NightWatch (3rd edition)* by Terence Dickinson (Firefly Books)
- *Celestial Delights* by Francis Reddy and Greg Walz-Chojnacki (Celestial Arts)
- *Star-Hopping for Backyard Astronomers* by Alan M. MacRobert (Sky Publishing)
- *The Beginner's Observing Guide* by Leo Enright (Royal Astronomical Society of Canada)
- *Touring the Universe through Binoculars* by Philip S. Harrington (Wiley)
- *Binocular Astronomy* by Craig Crossen (Willmann-Bell)
- *Turn Left at Orion* by Guy Consolmagno and Dan M. Davis (Cambridge University Press)
- *Celestial Objects for Modern Telescopes* by Michael A. Covington (Cambridge University Press)
- *Deep-Sky Companions: The Messier Objects* by Stephen James O'Meara (Sky Publishing)
- *How to Use a Computerized Telescope* by Michael A. Covington (Cambridge University Press)
- *Stars & Planets* by Ian Ridpath and Wil Tirion (Princeton University Press)
- *The Backyard Astronomer's Guide (revised edition)* by Terence Dickinson and Alan Dyer (Firefly Books)
- *The Deep Sky: An Introduction* by Philip S. Harrington (Sky Publishing)
- *Peterson Field Guide to the Stars and Planets* by Jay M. Pasachoff (Houghton Mifflin)
- *Observer's Handbook* (Royal Astronomical Society of Canada, annual publication)
- *SkyWatch* (Sky Publishing, annual publication)

Atlases and Star Charts
- *Bright Star Atlas 2000.0* by Wil Tirion and Brian Skiff (Willmann-Bell)
- *Norton's Star Atlas (20th edition)*, edited by Ian Ridpath (Pi Press)
- *DeepMap 600 Folding Star Chart* by Wil Tirion (Orion Telescopes and Binoculars)
- *Atlas of the Moon* by Antonín Rükl (Sky Publishing)
- *Sky Atlas 2000.0* by Wil Tirion and Roger Sinnott (Cambridge University Press)

Astrophotography
- *Astrophotography for the Amateur (2nd edition)* by Michael A. Covington (Cambridge University Press)
- *Practical Astrophotography* by Jeffrey R. Charles (Springer-Verlag)
- *Wide-Field Astrophotography* by Robert Reeves (University of Alabama Center for Business)
- *Photoshop for Astrophotographers* by Jerry Lodriguss (Astropix LLC)

General Interest
- *The Universe and Beyond (3rd edition)* by Terence Dickinson (Firefly Books)
- *Aurora: The Mysterious Northern Lights* by Candace Savage (Firefly Books)
- *The Modern Moon* by Charles A. Wood (Sky Publishing)
- *Glorious Eclipses* by Serge Brunier and Jean-Pierre Luminet (Cambridge University Press)
- *Meteorites: A Journey Through Space and Time* by Alex Bevan and John de Laeter (Smithsonian Books)
- *The New Solar System (4th edition)* by J. Kelly Beatty, Carolyn C. Petersen, and Andrew Chaikin (Cambridge University Press)
- *Deep-Sky Wonders* by Walter Scott Houston (Sky Publishing)
- *The Great Atlas of the Stars* by Serge Brunier and Akira Fujii (Firefly Books)
- *Astronomy Encyclopedia* edited by Patrick Moore (Oxford University Press)

Magazines:
- *Astronomy* (Kalmbach Publishing)
- *Night Sky* (Sky Publishing)
- *Sky & Telescope* (Sky Publishing)
- *Mercury* (Astronomical Society of the Pacific)
- *SkyNews* (SkyNews Inc.)
- *Astronomy & Space* (National Astronomy Club of Ireland)
- *Astronomy Now* (Pole Star Publications)
- *StarDate* (University of Texas McDonald Observatory)

APPENDIX

Listed here are dates (to 2015) and times for viewing occultations, eclipses, conjunctions, and more. The data is accurate for the Northern Hemisphere only, at mid-northern latitudes (as per the Sky Maps in Chapter Six).

Where and When to Find the Planets

Look for the planets along the ecliptic and in the zodiacal constellations.
In the listings, *nv* means the planet is not visible; it's too close to the Sun to be easily seen.

Mercury

	In the west after sunset	In the east before sunrise
2005	first half of Mar, first half of Jul	last half of Aug most of Dec
2006	last half of Feb, most of Jun	first half of Aug, late Nov to mid-Dec
2007	first half of Feb, late May to early Jun	most of Mar, last half of Jul, first half of Nov
2008	most of Jan, first half of May, mid-Sep, late Dec	mid-Mar, late Jun to mid-Jul, last half of Oct
2009	early Jan, last half of Apr, most of Aug, last half of Dec	most of Feb, all of Jun, first half of Oct
2010	first half of Apr, last half of Jul to early Aug, late Nov	mid-Jan to early Feb, late May, last half of Sep
2011	most of Mar, first half of Jul, mid-Nov	most of Jan, mid-May, first half of Sep, last half of Dec
2012	late Feb to mid-Mar, mid-Jun to early Jul, last half of Oct	mid-Apr to early May, most of Aug, late Nov to late Dec
2013	most of Feb, late May to late Jun	late Mar to early Apr, late Jul to early Aug, last half of Nov
2014	mid-Jan to early Feb, all of May, early to late Sep	late Feb to late Mar, most of Jul, late Oct to early Nov
2015	most of Jan, late Apr to mid-May, late Dec	early Feb to early Mar, late Jun to early Jul, early to late Oct

Venus

2005	to mid-Feb in the east before sunrise; *nv*; early May to year-end in the west after sunset
2006	late Jan to mid-Sept in the east before sunrise; *nv*; mid-Dec in the west after sunset
2007	to late Jul in the west after sunset; *nv*; late Aug to year-end in the east before sunrise
2008	to late Mar in the east before sunrise; *nv*; early Jul to year-end in the west after sunset
2009	to mid-Mar in the west after sunset; *nv*; early Apr to late Nov in the east before sunrise; *nv*
2010	late Feb to early Oct in the west after sunset; *nv*; early Nov to year-end in the east before sunrise
2011	to early Jul in the east before sunrise; *nv*; mid-Oct to year-end in the west after sunset
2012	to late May in the west after sunset; *nv*; mid-Jun to year-end in the east before sunrise
2013	to late Jan in the east before sunrise; *nv*; late Apr to year-end in the west after sunset
2014	mid-Jan to mid-Sep in the east before sunrise; *nv*; late Dec in the west after sunset
2015	to late Jul in the west after sunset; *nv*; early Sep to year-end in the east before sunrise

Location of Mars at mid-month

	2005	2006	2007	2008	2009	2010	2011	2012	2013	2014	2015
Jan	Oph	Ari	Sgr	Tau	*nv*	Cnc	*nv*	Vir	Cap	Vir	Aqr
Feb	Sgr	Tau	Sgr	Tau	Cap	Cnc	*nv*	Leo	Aqr	Vir	Psc
Mar	Sgr	Tau	Cap	Gem	Aqr	Cnc	*nv*	Leo	*nv*	Vir	Psc
Apr	Cap	Gem	Aqr	Gem	Aqr	Cnc	Psc	Leo	*nv*	Vir	Ari
May	Aqr	Gem	Psc	Cnc	Psc	Leo	Ari	Leo	*nv*	Vir	*nv*
Jun	Psc	Cnc	Psc	Leo	Ari	Leo	Tau	Leo	Tau	Vir	*nv*
Jul	Psc	Leo	Ari	Leo	Tau	Leo	Tau	Vir	Gem	Vir	*nv*
Aug	Ari	Leo	Tau	Vir	Tau	Vir	Gem	Vir	Gem	Lib	Cnc
Sep	Ari	*nv*	Tau	Vir	Cnc	Vir	Cnc	Lib	Cnc	Sco	Leo
Oct	Ari	*nv*	Gem	*nv*	Gem	Lib	Cnc	Sco	Leo	Oph	Leo
Nov	Ari	*nv*	Gem	*nv*	Cnc	Oph	Leo	Sgr	Leo	Sgr	Vir
Dec	Ari	Sco	Gem	*nv*	Leo	Sgr	Leo	Sgr	Vir	Cap	Vir

Jupiter

2005   In Virgo to late Sep; *nv*, and Nov; in Libra from late Nov on

2006   In Libra to late Oct; *nv*; in Scorpius from mid-Dec on

2007   In Ophiuchus to late Nov; *nv*

2008   In Sagittarius from late Jan on

2009   *nv*; in Capricornus from mid-Feb on

2010   In Aquarius to early Feb; *nv*; and Apr; in Pisces from May on

2011   In Pisces to mid-Mar; *nv*; and in late Apr to May; in Aries from Jun on

2012   In Aries to late Apr; *nv*; in Taurus from early Jun on

2013   In Taurus until early Jun; *nv*; in Gemini from early Jul on

2014   In Gemini until early Jul; *nv*; in Cancer in mid-Aug to Sep; in Leo from Oct on

2015   In Leo in Jan; in Cancer from Feb to May; in Leo in Jun to early Aug; *nv*; and mid-Sep on

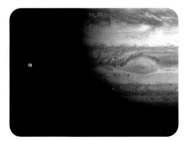

Saturn

2005   In Gemini until early Jul; *nv*; in Cancer from early Aug on

2006   In Cancer until mid-Jul; *nv*; in Leo from late Aug on

2007   In Leo until early Aug; *nv*; and from early Sep on

2008   In Leo until mid-Aug; *nv*; and from mid-Sep on

2009   In Leo until late Aug; *nv*; in Virgo from early Oct on

2010   In Virgo until early Sep; *nv*; and from mid-Oct on

2011   In Virgo until mid-Sep; *nv*; and from late Oct on

2012   In Virgo until early Oct; *nv*; in Libra from Nov on

2013   In Libra until May; in Virgo from Jun to Aug; in Libra from Sept to mid-Oct; *nv*; and from late Nov on

2014   In Libra until late Oct; *nv*; and from early Dec on

2015   In Scorpius until May; in Libra from Jun to early Nov; *nv*

Transits of Mercury and Venus 2005–2015

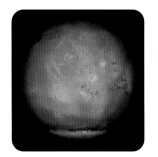

Mercury
   November 8, 2006
Venus
   June 5–6, 2012

Mars at Opposition 2005–2015

Date	Constellation	Magnitude
November 7, 2005	Aries	−2.3
December 24, 2007	Gemini	−1.6
January 29, 2010	Cancer	−1.3
March 3, 2012	Leo	−1.2
April 8, 2014	Virgo	−1.5

Occultations of the Planets by the Moon 2005–2015

As with eclipses, you have to be in the right place to see an occultation. Just as you won't see a total eclipse if you're not in the path of totality, you won't see an occultation if you're outside its region of visibility. (You also won't see the occultation if it happens during the day.) We've listed most of the major events here, however, because, even if you can't see the occultation, the planet and the Moon will appear beautifully close together in the nighttime sky on the date of the event. (This will create a great photo opportunity: see Chapter Eleven.) Occultations of Uranus and Neptune are not here; while they do occur, they're challenging to observe.

2005

January 4	Jupiter
January 31	Jupiter
February 27	Jupiter
March 26	Jupiter
April 22	Jupiter
May 19	Jupiter
May 31	Mars
June 16	Jupiter
July 13	Jupiter
August 7	Venus
August 10	Jupiter
September 7	Venus
December 12	Mars

2006

April 24	Venus
July 27	Mars
August 25	Mars
December 10	Saturn

2007

January 6	Saturn
January 20	Venus
February 2–3	Saturn
March 2	Saturn
March 17	Mercury
March 29	Saturn
April 14	Mars
April 25	Saturn
May 22	Saturn
June 18	Venus
June 19	Saturn
July 16	Saturn
September 10	Saturn
October 7	Saturn
December 23–24	Mars

2008

January 19	Mars
March 5	Mercury
March 5	Venus
April 12	Mars
May 10	Mars
June 8	Mars
December 1	Venus
December 29	Mercury
December 29	Jupiter

2009

February 22	Mercury
February 23	Jupiter
February 28	Venus
April 22	Venus
September 13	Mars
October 12	Mars

2010

May 16	Venus
September 11	Venus

2011

July 27	Mars
October 28	Mercury

2012

June 17	Jupiter
July 15	Jupiter
August 11	Jupiter
August 13	Venus
September 8	Jupiter
September 19	Mars
October 5	Jupiter
October 16	Mercury
November 2	Jupiter
November 28	Jupiter
December 12	Mercury
December 25	Jupiter

2013

January 21	Jupiter
February 18	Jupiter
September 8	Venus
December 1	Saturn
December 1	Mercury
December 29	Saturn

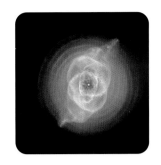

Major Planetary Gatherings 2005–2015

2005

January 13	Mercury/Venus
June 25	Venus/Saturn
June 27	Mercury/Venus
September 1	Venus/Jupiter
September 6	Moon/Venus/Jupiter
October 5	Mercury/Jupiter

2006

June 16	Mars/Saturn
June 27	Moon/Mercury/ Saturn/Mars
August 10	Venus/Mercury
August 20	Mercury/Saturn
August 26	Venus/Saturn
October 21	Mercury/Jupiter
December 9	Mercury/Mars/Jupiter
December 18	Moon/Jupiter/ Mars/Mercury

2007

February 4	Venus/Mercury
June 30	Venus/Saturn
October 14	Venus/Saturn

2008

February 1	Venus/Jupiter
February 4	Moon/Venus/Jupiter
February 26	Mercury/Venus
March 23	Mercury/Venus
July 9	Mars/Saturn
August 13	Venus/Saturn
August 15	Mercury/Saturn
August 19	Mercury/Venus
September 1	Moon/Venus/ Mercury/Mars
September 7	Mercury/Venus/Mars
December 1	Moon/Venus/Jupiter
December 30	Mercury/Jupiter

2009

February 17	Mars/Jupiter
February 22	Moon/Mercury/ Jupiter/Mars
March 1	Mercury/Mars
April 22	Venus/Mars
June 19	Venus/Mars
August 17	Mercury/Saturn
October 8	Mercury/Saturn
October 13	Venus/Saturn
October 16	Moon/Venus/ Saturn/Mercury

2010

February 16	Venus/Jupiter
April 5	Venus/Mercury
July 30	Mars/Saturn
August 8	Venus/Saturn
August 12	Moon/Venus/Mars/ Mercury/Saturn
August 20	Venus/Mars
November 19	Mercury/Mars

2011

March 14	Mercury/Jupiter
May 1	Moon/Venus/Mercury/ Jupiter/Mars
May 9	Mercury/Venus/ Jupiter/Mars
May 11	Venus/Jupiter
May 19	Mercury/Venus/Mars
May 23	Venus/Mars
May 30	Moon/Venus/Jupiter/ Mars/Mercury
October 30	Venus/Mercury

2012

February 26	Moon/Jupiter/Venus
March 12	Venus/Jupiter
March 25	Moon/Jupiter/Venus
March 26	Moon/Venus/Jupiter

(Occultations continued from previous page)

2014

January 25	Saturn
February 21	Saturn
February 26	Venus
March 21	Saturn
April 17	Saturn
May 14	Saturn
June 10	Saturn
July 5	Mars
July 7	Saturn
August 4	Saturn
August 31	Saturn
September 28	Saturn
October 25	Saturn

2015

March 21	Mars
June 15	Mercury
July 19	Venus
October 8	Venus
October 11	Mercury
December 6	Mars
December 7	Venus

(Gatherings continued on next page)

(Gatherings continued from previous page)

June 17	Moon/Jupiter/Venus
June 30	Venus/Jupiter
July 15	Moon/Jupiter/Venus
August 14	Mars/Saturn
October 4	Mercury/Saturn
November 26	Venus/Saturn
December 9	Venus/Mercury

2013

February 8	Mercury/Mars
May 25	Mercury/Venus/Jupiter
May 28	Venus/Jupiter
June 19	Mercury/Venus
July 22	Mars/Jupiter
September 17	Venus/Saturn
October 7	Moon/Venus/ Saturn/Mercury
November 25	Mercury/Saturn

2014

July 16	Venus/Mercury
August 18	Venus/Jupiter
August 23	Moon/Venus/Jupiter
August 25	Mars/Saturn

2015

January 10	Mercury/Venus
February 21	Venus/Mars
April 22	Mercury/Mars
June 19	Moon/Venus/Jupiter
June 30	Venus/Jupiter
July 18	Moon/Venus/Jupiter
August 6	Mercury/Jupiter
October 9	Moon/Venus/ Jupiter/Mars
October 17	Mars/Jupiter
October 25	Venus/Jupiter
November 2	Venus/Mars
November 6	Moon/Venus/ Jupiter/Mars

Solar Eclipses: 2005–2015

Date	Type	Where Visible
April 8–9, 2005	Annular/Total	Pacific Ocean, Panama, Columbia
October 3, 2005	Annular	Portugal, Spain, Libya, Sudan, Kenya
March 29, 2006	Total	Ghana, Niger, Libya, Turkey, Russia
September 22, 2006	Annular	NE South America, Atlantic Ocean
March 19, 2007	Partial	central and eastern Asia, western Alaska
September 11, 2007	Partial	southern South America
February 7, 2008	Annular	Antarctica
August 1, 2008	Total	northern Canada, Greenland, Siberia, Mongolia, China
January 26, 2009	Annular	southern Indian Ocean, Sumatra, Borneo
July 22, 2009	Total	India, Nepal, China, Pacific Ocean
January 15, 2010	Annular	Zaire, Kenya, southern India, central China
July 11, 2010	Total	South Pacific, Easter Island, southern Chile and Argentina
January 4, 2011	Partial	Europe, northern Africa, southern Asia
June 1, 2011	Partial	northeast Asia, northern Alaska and Canada, Iceland
July 1, 2011	Partial	southern Atlantic and Indian Oceans
November 25, 2011	Partial	southern Africa and New Zealand, Tasmania
May 20-21, 2012	Annular	southeast China, Japan, Pacific, western and southwestern United States
November 13, 2012	Total	northern Australia, South Pacific
May 9-10, 2013	Annular	northern Australia, Solomon Islands, central Pacific
November 3, 2013	Annular/Total	Atlantic, Gabon, Congo, Zaire
April 29, 2014	Annular	Antarctica
October 23, 2014	Partial	North Pacific, North America
March 20, 2015	Total	North Atlantic, Faeroe Islands, Svalbard
September 13, 2015	Partial	southern Africa, southern Indian Ocean, Antarctica

Lunar Eclipses: 2005-2015

(Penumbral eclipses are not included, as the darkening of the Moon is usually too faint to be easily seen.)

Date	Type	Where Visible
October 17, 2005	Partial	Australia, New Zealand, eastern Asia, northwestern North America
September 7–8, 2006	Partial	eastern Europe and Africa, Asia, Australia
March 3–4, 2007	Total	eastern North America, most of South America, Europe, Africa, central Asia; partial in central North America, eastern Australia, Far East
August 28, 2007	Total	most of the United States, New Zealand, Australia, Japan. Partial in China
February 20–21, 2008	Total	North and South America, Europe, most of Africa; partial in central Asia
August 16–17, 2008	Partial	Africa, most of Europe, Asia, Australia, South America
December 31, 2009	Partial	Europe, Asia, Africa, Australia
June 26, 2010	Partial	Hawaii, western Alaska, New Zealand, Australia
December 21, 2010	Total	North and South America, western Europe, New Zealand; partial in western Africa, most of Australia and the Far East
June 15–16, 2011	Total	Europe, Africa, eastern Australia, India, China; partial in eastern South America, eastern Australia
December 10, 2011	Total	northwestern North America, Australia, Asia; partial in the rest of North America, Europe
June 4, 2012	Partial	western North America, Hawaii, Australia, New Zealand
April 25–26, 2013	Partial	central Africa, Asia
April 15, 2014	Total	North and South America, eastern Australia; partial in western Africa
October 8, 2014	Total	most of North America, Australia, Far East; partial in northeastern North America, South America, central Asia
April 4, 2015	Total	western North America, New Zealand, Australia, Far East; partial in eastern North America, western South America, India
September 27–28, 2015	Total	North and South America, Europe; partial in Alaska, western Russia, Middle East

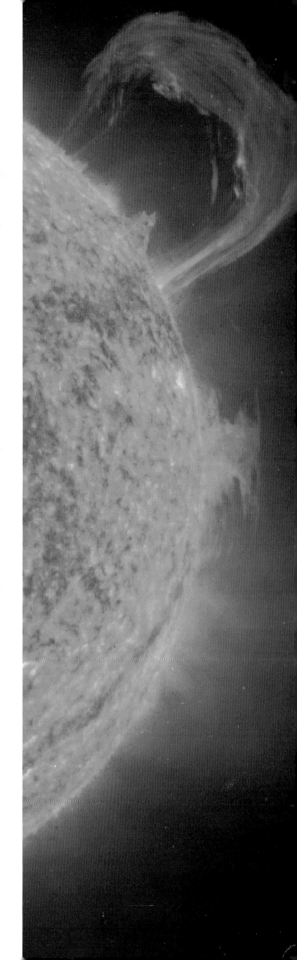

INDEX

elongation, 41
Epsilon Boötis. 86
Epsilon Lyrae, 90

Fomalhaut, 90

galaxies, 68–70, *68, 69, 70*
    Andromeda, 70, 92, *92*
    Clouds of Magellan, *70, 149*
    elliptical, 70
    irregular, 70
    projects, 71
    Sombrero, 68
    spiral, 68
Galileo, 26, 42
Great Red Spot, *see* Jupiter
Great Square (Pegasus), 90
Greek alphabet, 74

Horseshoe Nebula, *see* M17
Hubble Space Telescope, 105
Hyades, 94

International Space Station,
    105, *140*
Iridium flare, 106, *106,* 140

Jupiter, *34,* 35, 42–43, *42, 43*
    Great Red Spot, *34,* 42,
        42
    moons, 42, *42*
    when and where to find,
        157

Keystone (Hercules), 86

Kuiper Belt, 13, 47, 98, 103

Lagoon Nebula, *see* M8
light pollution, 20–21
light-year, 12
Little Dipper, 84, *84*
lunar eclipses, *see* eclipses,
    lunar

M1, 67
M4, 86
M5, 86
M6, 88
M7, 88
M8, 88
M11, 90
M13, 86, *86*
M15, 90
M17, *66,* 88
M20, 88
M22, 88
M23, 88
M24, 88
M25, 88
M27, 90, *90*
M31, 70, 92, *92*
M35, *62,* 84
M36, 94
M37, 94
M38, 94
M41, 94
M42, 66, 94
M44, 84
M45, 94, *94*
M46, 95

M47, 94
M57, *83,* 90
M80, *64*
M92, 86
magnitude scale, 65
Mare, 26, *27, 28, 29*
Mars, 39–41, *39*
    features, 39, 40–41
    moons, 41
    opposition, 39, *40,* 158
    when and where to find,
        157
measuring distances, 78
Melotte 111, *64,* 86
Mercury, 35–36, *35,*
    Transit of, 158
    when and where to find,
        156
Messier Catalog, 70
Messier, Charles, 70
meteor showers
    dates of, 105
    Delta Aquarids, 89
    Eta Aquarids, 87
    Geminids, 93
    Leonids, 93
    Lyrids, 85
    Orionids, 91
    Perseids, 89
    project, 107
    Quadrantids, 95
    radiant, 104
    Taurids, 93
meteors, 102–105, *139*
    observing, 104

Milky Way, 12, 13, 68, 88, 144
Mirfak, 92
Mizar, 84
Moon, 22–33
    eclipses, 114
    features, 26–30
    formation, 22–23
    lunar cycle, 24–25
    map, 28–29
    occultations, 30
    origin, 23
    phases, 24–25
    projects, 32–33
    shooting, 145, *145*
Moon illusion, 31, 32

Near-Earth Objects (NEOs),
    49
New General Catalogue
    (NGC), 70
nebulas, *61,* 66–67, 88, 94
    dark, 67, *67*
    emission, 66, *66*
    reflection, 66, *66*
    planetary, 66-67, *66*
    supernova remnants, 67,
        67

Neptune, 46–47, *47,* 49
    moons, 47, 49
Northern Cross, 88
North Star, *see* Polaris

observing log, 18, 19
observing tips, 15–16

PHOTOGRAPHY & ILLUSTRATION CREDITS

All photographs by Alan Dyer, except for the following:

Page 46 (bottom), Dr. R. Albrecht, ESA/ESO Space Telescope European Coordinating Facility; NASA

Pages 41, 42 (center), 44 (bottom), 58, 59, Jeff Ball, www.earthandskyphoto.com

Page 11, By special permission of the City of Bayeux

Pages 18 (bottom), 121, 127 (left), 128 (both), 130, Courtesy Celestron International

Pages 10 (top), 17 (top), 55, 56, 73, 129 (top), 140, Paul Deans

Pages 20 (bottom), 48, 133, Dennis di Cicco

Page 40 (top), Richard Tresch Feinberg

Pages 98 (bottom), 102, 146, Johnny Horne

Pages 64 (bottom), 66 (bottom right), 70 (top, right), 83 (left), Hubble Heritage Team (STScI/AURA/NASA)

Page 101 (left), Hubble Space Telescope Comet Team and NASA

Page 10 (bottom), Courtesy of H.R. MacMillan Space Centre

Page 21, Craig Mayhew and Robert Simmon, NASA GSFC

Page 127 (center), Courtesy of Meade Instruments Corporation

Page 69, NASA, ESA, S. Beckwith (STScI), and the HUDF Team

Page 159 (top), NASA, ESA, HEIC, and the Hubble Heritage Team (STScI/AURA)

Page 66 (center spread), NASA, ESA, and J. Hester (ASU)

Pages 60, 61, 159 (bottom), NASA, ESA, and the Hubble Heritage Team (STScI/AURA)

Page 67 (bottom, right), NASA, H. Ford (JHU), G. Illingworth (UCSC/LO), M. Clampin (STScI), G. Hartig (STScI), the ACS Science Team, and ESA

Page 6 (inset, left center), NASA and the Hubble Heritage Team

Pages 45, 63, 66 (bottom left), 67 (bottom, left), 68, NASA and the Hubble Heritage Team (STScI/AURA)

118 (bottom), NASA Johnson Space Center (NASA-JSC)

Pages 42 (bottom), 46 (top), 47, NASA/JPL

Pages 39, 40 (bottom), 158, NASA/JPL/Malin Space Science Systems

Pages 34, 44 (top), 157 (bottom), NASA/JPL/Space Science Institute

Pages 42 (top), 157 (top), NASA/JPL/University of Arizona

Page 64 (top), NASA, C.R. O'Dell, and S.K. Wong (Rice University)

Page 37, Damian Peach

Page 57, Royal Swedish Academy of Sciences

Page 31, Kevin Sato

Pages 22, 25 (top), 26, 27, 28, 29, Gary Seronik

Pages 52, 53, 161, Courtesy of SOHO/Extreme Ultraviolet Imaging Telescope (EIT) consortium

Page 83 (right), Adam Stuart

Page 118 (top), J.T. Trauger (Jet Propulsion Laboratory) and NASA

Pages 127 (right), 129 (bottom), 131, Courtesy of Orion Telescopes & Binoculars, www.telescope.com

Page 139, Jimmy Westlake

All illustrations by Judy Love, except for the following:
Page 19, Becky Ramotowski

ACKNOWLEDGMENTS

I have always wanted to write a book—and have it published. That I have been able to achieve this is due in no small part to several people. My sincere thanks:

To Holly Harrison, who opened the Rockport door for me. Your generosity, moral support, and helpful advice are deeply appreciated.

To the wonderful folks at Rockport, who made this book a reality: Betsy Gammons, Delilah Smittle, and especially Winnie Prentiss—thank you for this opportunity!

To Sally McGillivray and Susan Lit at Sky Publishing, for supplying us with the terrific Sky Maps—they add so much!

To Ken Hewitt-White, who checked for potentially embarrassing errors (and there were a few!).

To all of the photographers and illustrators who contributed their amazing images to this book. Their credits are listed on page 166.

To Paul Deans, whose help and support in producing this book was immeasurable. I could not have done it without you!

ABOUT THE AUTHOR

Pat Price is a writer and former magazine editor, who has written on several subjects, including travel, health, home and garden, and science. She also spent several years as a writer/producer with the Edmonton Space Sciences Centre (now the Odysseum) in Alberta, Canada. A resident of the United States since 2000, Pat lives with her amateur astronomer husband and aging cat in Arlington, Massachusetts. This is her first book.